WARRIORS

OF

ROME

An Illustrated Military History of the Roman Legions

MICHAEL SIMKINS

Colour plates by James Field

BLANDFORD

Blandford
an imprint of Cassell
Villiers House, 41–47 Strand, London WC2N 5JE

Text copyright © 1988 Michael Simkins

Distributed in the United States by
Sterling Publishing Co. Inc.
387 Park Avenue South, New York, NY 10016-8810

Distributed in Australia by
Capricorn Link (Australia) Pty Ltd
PO Box 665, Lane Cove, NSW 2066

First published 1988
Hardback reprinted 1989, 1990
Paperback first published 1989
Reprinted 1990, 1992

British Library Cataloguing in Publication Data

Simkins, Michael
Warriors of Rome: an illustrated history
of the Roman legions.
1. Rome—Army—History
I. Title
355'.00937   U35

ISBN 0 7137 2001 8 hardback
ISBN 0 7137 2197 9 paperback

Typeset by Best-set Typesetter Ltd.

Printed in Hong Kong by Colorcraft Ltd.

WARRIORS
OF
ROME

This Book
belongs to the Library of
King Edward VI's
Grammar School,
Guildford, Surrey

Contents

Author's Note

Legions are numbered and named in this book in the original Latin form, e.g. LEGIO XX VALERIA.

Other Latin words and ancient place names, Roman and others, appear in *italics*. The name of the Catuvellaunian capital is given as *Camulodunon*, the original Celtic spelling, prior to the Roman invasion of Britain; the Romans subsequently altered the name to *Camulodunum*, when the town became their provincial capital.

A soldier's rank commences with a capital letter when a particular individual is referred to, e.g. *Centurio* Marcus Favonius Facilis. All Roman ranks appear in *italics*.

Who can wonder that in the east the Euphrates, in the west the ocean, in the south the richest plains of Africa, in the north the Danube and the Rhine are the limits of the Empire? One might say with truth that the conquests are less remarkable than the conquerors.

Flavius Josephus (Joseph ben Matthias), first century AD.

I passed on, making these reflections, to a dark arcade, overgrown with ilex. In the openings which time and violence have made, a distant grove of cypresses discover themselves, springing from heaps of mouldering ruins, relieved by a clear sky strewn with a few red clouds. This was the sort of prospect I desired, and I sat down on a shattered frieze to enjoy it. Many stories of ancient Rome thronged into my mind as I mused; triumphal scenes, but tempered by sadness, and the awful thoughts of their being all passed away...

William Beckford, 1783

Acknowledgements

The author wishes to express his sincere thanks to the following colleagues:

Dr Marcus Junkelmann, MA, for his interest and assistance in providing information upon the Weiler cavalry helmet and the Aquincum bronze legionary helmet;

Mr Trevor Cowie of the National Museum of the Antiquities of Scotland, for his assistance in the reconstruction of Roman field flasks;

The staff of the Joint Library of the Institute of Classical Studies, London, for their valuable assistance over a number of years;

Miss Fiona McKenzie for her help and advice in correcting numerous errors in the original manuscript;

James Field for his evocative colour plates.

Chronology

All names and nicknames of the recognised Emperors appearing in this chronology appear in **bold** type for ease of identification.

BC

- *c.* 157   Birth of Gaius Marius.
- 121   Rome annexes southern Gaul.
- 112   War is declared against King Jugurtha.
- 111   Lucius Calpurnius Bestia, the Roman commander, fails to overcome Jugurtha.
- 110   Bestia is replaced by Spurius and Aulus Postumius Albinus, who also fail against Jugurtha.
- 109   Command is given to Quintus Caecilius Metellus.
- 107   Marius is elected Consul and replaces Metellus in Numidia.
- 105   King Jugurtha is betrayed and captured by the Romans. He is put to death and the Jugurthine War closes. A large Roman force is defeated at *Arausio* (Orange) by the Cimbri and Teutones.
- 102   Marius defeats the Teutones at *Aquae Sextiae* (Aix-en-Provence).
- 101   Marius defeats the Cimbri on the Raudine plain in northern Italy and the Germanic threat is removed.
- *c.* 100   Birth of Gaius Julius Caesar.
- 88   Lucius Cornelius Sulla is elected Consul and causes Marius to seek refuge in North Africa. Sulla leaves Italy to recover eastern territories overrun by Mithridates, King of Pontus.
- 87   Marius returns to Rome and organises a massacre of his opponents. He dies during his seventh consulship in 86.
- 85   Sulla concludes a treaty with Mithridates.
- 83   Sulla returns to Rome and civil war breaks out.
- 81   Sulla is made *Dictator*. He retires to private life in 79 after introducing many reforms and dies in 78 at the age of 59.
- 71–70   A serious slave revolt led by the Thracian gladiator Spartacus is crushed by Marcus Licinius Crassus and Gnaeus Pompeius.
- 60   Crassus, Pompeius and Caesar form the unofficial First Triumvirate and Caesar is elected consul in 59.
- 58   Caesar prevents the Helvetii migrating to western Gaul and the conquest of Gaul begins.

55–54	Caesar makes raids into Britain.
53	Crassus is killed in battle against the Parthians.
51	The conquest of Gaul is completed.
49	Caesar moves against Pompeius and civil war commences.
48	Pompeius is defeated by Caesar at the battle of *Pharsalus* and escapes to *Alexandria* where he is assassinated.
47	The civil war continues under the direction of the supporters of Pompeius.
46–45	Caesar defeats the Pompeians at *Thapsus* in North Africa and at *Munda* in Spain.
44	Caesar is declared *Dictator in perpetuo* in February. His opponents plot against him and he is murdered in the Curia of the Senate on 15 March. Marcus Antonius takes control in Rome, but the chief persons involved in Caesar's murder, Brutus and Cassius, evade capture and flee Italy. Gaius Julius Caesar Octavianus, grand-nephew of the Dictator, gains the support of the Senate in opposition to Antonius.
43	Octavianus defeats Antonius at the battle of *Mutina* and Antonius retreats to southern Gaul. The two men come to terms later in the year and together with the chief priest, Marcus Aemilius Lepidus, they form the (officially recognised) Second Triumvirate.
42	The conspirators, Brutus and Cassius, are defeated in battle at *Philippi* and both commit suicide.
36	Antonius campaigns against the Parthians.
33	The rivalry between Octavianus and Antonius returns and in 32 the breach becomes irreconcilable, largely because of Antonius' association with the ambitious Queen Cleopatra of Egypt.
31	The marine forces of Antonius and Cleopatra are defeated off *Actium* by Octavianus' naval commander, Marcus Vipsanius Agrippa.
30	Octavianus invades Egypt and both Antonius and Cleopatra commit suicide. Octavianus becomes the sole ruler of the Roman world.
27	Octavianus takes the titles of *Imperator* and **Augustus**; though outwardly expressing Republican sympathies, he in fact becomes the first Roman Emperor.
25	Rome annexes *Galatia*.
16–15	Augustus' stepsons, Tiberius and Nero Drusus, annex the provinces of *Noricum* and *Raetia*.
12	Marcus Vipsanius Agrippa dies.

Birth of Christ (Anno Domini)

9   Three legions and their auxiliaries are massacred in the Teutoburg Forest by the German chieftain Arminius.

14   Augustus dies and is succeeded by his stepson **Tiberius** Claudius Nero. The Rhine and Pannonian legions mutiny against harsh conditions.

14–16   Germanicus campaigns against the Germans east of the Rhine to the river Elbe.

37   Tiberius dies and is succeeded by his grand-nephew Gaius Caesar (**Caligula**).

39   An army plot against Gaius Caesar is discovered and suppressed by the Emperor. Already mentally unhinged, possibly as a result of plumbism, Gaius Caesar becomes even more erratic and murderous.

41   Officers of the Praetorian Guard assassinate the Emperor and he is replaced by his uncle Tiberius **Claudius** Drusus.

43   Four legions invade Britain.

54   Claudius dies; probably murdered by his wife, Agrippina the Younger, to secure the succession for her son **Nero** Claudius Caesar Drusus Germanicus.

58–60   General Gnaeus Domitius Corbulo undertakes campaigns against the Parthians.

60   Governor Gaius Suetonius Paullinus destroys the Druidic centre on *Mona Insula* (Anglesey). The tribes of southern Britain rebel under the leadership of Queen Boudica.

61   Paullinus defeats Boudica in battle, probably at *Manduessedum* (Mancetter).

66   General Flavius Sabinus Vespasianus is sent to Judaea to put down a serious rebellion.

68   Governor of Central Gaul, Gaius Julius Vindex, rebels against Nero, but is killed in battle at *Vesontio* (Besançon) by the Governor of Upper Germany.

Governor of Nearer Spain, **Sulpicius Galba**, also rises against Nero; with the support of the Senate, he enrolls LEGIO VII GALBIANA and marches on Rome. Nero commits suicide and Galba succeeds him. Galba becomes unpopular immediately.

69   The Year of the Four Caesars. The legions of Upper Germany demand the replacement of Galba. The legions of Lower Germany elect their own Governor, Aulus Vitellius, as Emperor.

Galba chooses his own successor to secure his position, but is murdered by Marcus Salvius Otho, who had helped him in the early stages of his revolt.

Otho succeeds as Emperor, but is defeated by Vitellius at the first battle of *Bedriacum*, near *Cremona*. Otho commits suicide and **Vitellius** succeeds him.

The eastern legions declare for Vespasianus and the forces of Vitellius are defeated at the second battle of *Bedriacum* by Vespasianus' general, Marcus Antonius Primus. Vitellius is put to death.

A revolt on the Rhine, led by Julius Civilis, loses Roman control of the Lower German province, but it is recovered shortly after by Quintus Petillius Cerealis and Annius Gallus. **Vespasianus** is declared Emperor by the Senate and the civil war ends.

70   The Jewish War of 66 ends with the fall of Jerusalem. Remnants of the Zealot forces retire to strongholds in southern Judaea.

72   Governor Flavius Silva is sent to invest the last remaining rebels who hold the Herodian fortress of *Masada*.

73   The defenders of *Masada* commit suicide, rather than capitulate.

79   Vespasianus dies and is succeeded by his son **Titus**.

81   Titus dies at the age of 42, possibly murdered by his brother Titus Flavius **Domitianus**, who becomes Emperor.

85–86   Domitianus campaigns unsuccessfully against the Dacians.

88   A further campaign against the Dacians leads to Roman success at *Tapae*, though Domitianus fails to exploit the advantage.

89   Governor of Upper Germany, Antonius Saturninus, rebels against Domitianus, but is quickly brought to battle on the plain of Andernach by the Governor of Lower Germany and defeated.

96   Officers of the Praetorian Guard conspire with the Emperor's wife, Domitia, and he is murdered. He is succeeded by the 66-year-old Marcus Cocceius **Nerva**, who adopts Marcus Ulpius Trajanus as his heir.

98   Nerva dies and **Trajanus** becomes Emperor.

101–106   Trajanus undertakes two successful campaigns against the Dacians and their King, Decebalus, commits suicide. Rome annexes *Dacia*.

114   Rome annexes *Armenia*. Trajanus attempts to annex Mesopotamia.

115–116   Trajanus advances to the Persian Gulf, but Jewish revolts in the eastern provinces and raids by the Parthians oblige him to withdraw.

117   Trajanus dies. He is succeeded by Publius Aelius **Hadrianus**.

120   The construction of the great defence works in northern Britain, known as Hadrian's Wall, may have commenced in this year.

122   Hadrianus visits the province of Britain.

132   The Second Jewish War commences under the leadership of Bar Kosiba.

135	The Jewish War is concluded.
138	Hadrianus dies and the succession passes to Titus Aelius Hadrianus Antoninus, later titled **Antoninus Pius**.
141	The northern frontier in Britain is advanced to the Forth–Clyde line, known as the Antonine Wall.
161	Antoninus Pius dies and his adopted nephew **Marcus** Aelius **Aurelius** Verus succeeds. In the second half of this decade, a serious plague devastates the Roman world.
170–175	Marcus Aurelius campaigns on the Danube and against the Sarmatians. A revolt by Avidius Cassius in Syria prevents conclusive victory.
177–178	Marcus Aurelius undertakes further campaigns on the Danube, but is unable to complete the consolidation of the frontier before his death in 180.
180	Lucius Aelius Aurelius **Commodus**, the dissolute son of Marcus Aurelius, becomes Emperor and terminates his father's efforts to quell barbarian incursions by force of arms.
186	An army revolt in Britain is put down by Publius Helvius Pertinax.
192	Commodus is assassinated on the last day of the year.
193	Publius Helvius **Pertinax** is forced to become Emperor, but is murdered by members of the Praetorian Guard three months later.

Marcus **Didius** Salvius **Julianus** purchases the position of Emperor at an auction and is killed shortly thereafter. Civil war breaks out with three candidates for the purple supported by their legions: Gaius Pescennius Niger in Syria, Decimus Clodius Ceironius Septimius Albinus in Britain and Lucius **Septimius Severus** on the Danube. |
194	Albinus is recognised as heir by Severus until Niger's claim has been negated. Severus defeats Niger and he is put to death with his family. Albinus attempts to overthrow Severus.
197	Albinus is brought to battle at Lyons and is defeated by Severus, who assumes total supremacy. Repairs to the northern defence works in Britain, seriously damaged by barbarian incursions during the civil war, are begun.
205	Rebuilding works in northern Britain are completed.
208	Severus undertakes an extensive campaign in Scotland.
211	Severus dies before the end of the campaign and it is probably completed by his son, Marcus Aurelius Antoninus, nicknamed **Caracalla**, who succeeds his father in joint power with his brother, Lucius Septimius **Geta**.
212	Roman citizenship is granted to all free-born subjects within the Empire. Caracalla arranges his brother's murder and becomes sole ruler.
217	Caracalla is murdered by Marcus Opelius Severus **Macrinus**,

who succeeds him. Macrinus campaigns unsuccessfully against the Parthians.

218   After defeat in battle against Caracalla's cousin Marcus Aurelius Antoninus, known as **Elagabalus** or **Heliogabalus**, Macrinus is killed and Elagabalus succeeds, though under domination of his grandmother Julia Maesa and his mother Julia Soaemias.

222   Elagabalus proves weak and promiscuous, alienating the Senate. Julia Maesa conspires with her daughter Julia Mamaea and bribes the Praetorian Guard to murder Elagabalus, in favour of Mamaea's son, **Severus Alexander**. Mamaea effectively rules through her son, aged 14 at his accession.

231   Severus Alexander and Mamaea repel a Sassanid Persian invasion of Mesopotamia.

235   The Emperor and his mother return to counter a German threat on the Rhine, but are both killed by army officers.
The Rhine legions proclaim Gaius Julius Verus Maximinus as Emperor **Maximinus I**, but the Senate declares him to be a public enemy and he is eventually killed by his own soldiers.

238   Marcus Antonius Gordianus succeeds as **Gordianus Africanus I** by the authority of the Senate, in joint power with his son Marcus Antonianus Gordianus, **Gordianus Africanus II**. The two men reign for little over a month; Gordianus I commits suicide upon learning of his son's death in battle against the Governor of Numidia, Capellianus.
Decimus Caelius **Balbinus** and Marcus Clodius **Pupienus** Maximus are appointed joint Emperors by the Senate, but are killed by the Praetorian Guard once Maximinus I has been eliminated by his own soldiers. The Praetorian Guard proclaims Marcus Antonius Gordianus, grandson of Gordianus I, Emperor **Gordianus III Pius**.

244   Marcus Julius Philippus, an officer of the Praetorian Guard, arranges the murder of Gordianus Pius and succeeds as **Philippus I**.

249   The Danube legions revolt against Philippus and force their commander, Gaius Messius Quintus **Trajanus Decius**, to take the title of Emperor. Decius engages Philippus in battle and the latter is killed.

251   Trajanus Decius is killed in battle by the Goths at the battle of *Abrittus*. The younger son of Decius, Gaius Valens **Hostilianus** Messius Quintus, is depicted on his coinage wearing an Imperial crown; however, very little is known of his apparently brief span.
The succession passes to Gaius Vibius **Trebonianus Gallus**. His reign, like that of Marcus Aurelius, sees a widespread serious plague, the nature of which remains unknown.

253 Governor Marcus Aemilius **Aemilianus** is proclaimed Emperor by the legions of *Pannonia* and *Moesia* and engages the forces of Gallus, defeating them despite support from Publius Licinius **Valerianus** whose army arrived too late to be of assistance. Both Aemilianus and Gallus are subsequently murdered by their own soldiers.

Valerianus and his son Publius Licinius Valerianus Egnatius **Gallienus** are proclaimed joint Emperors and continue to rule until 260 when, in an eastern border campaign, Valerianus is defeated and captured by the Persian King Shapur I: he is held prisoner until he dies.

259 Marcus Cassianus Latinius **Postumus**, Governor of Gaul, declares himself Emperor with widespread support in western Europe. He establishes a seat of government at Trier and rules effectively in Gaul, Spain and Britain.

265 Postumus appoints Marcus Piavonius **Victorinus** as co-Emperor.

267 Ulpius Cornelius Laelianus leads a revolt against Postumus, but fails and is killed. Postumus is killed in battle later in the year, fighting against the forces of the central government.

268 Gallienus is assassinated by his own soldiers. He is succeeded by Marcus Aurelius **Claudius II**, who achieves notable victories against the German tribe of the Alamanni which had penetrated into Italy and against the Goths in *Moesia*, which earned him the title of *Gothicus*.

270 Claudius II dies and is succeeded by Lucius Domitius **Aurelianus**, who completes the expulsion of the Goths. He then campaigns in Syria and Egypt. The massive defensive walls of Rome, which still stand today, were constructed in this reign.

275 Aurelianus is assassinated and Marcus Claudius **Tacitus** is proclaimed Emperor by the Senate, but is killed by his own soldiers six months later.

276 Marcus Annius **Florianus**, half-brother of Tacitus, assumes power after his death, but is killed in battle a few weeks later by Marcus Aurelius **Probus**, who had served with the armies of Valerianus, Claudius and Aurelianus.

282 Probus is killed by mutinous soldiers. Marcus Aurelius **Carus** is elected Emperor by the army. Carus appoints his two sons, **Carinus** and **Numerianus**, as Caesars.

283 Carus is killed while campaigning against the Persians; his death may have been caused by lightning. His younger son, Numerianus, dies or is killed shortly after him in 284, and Gaius Aurelius Valerius **Diocletianus** is proclaimed Emperor by his army.

285 Carinus defeats Diocletianus in battle, only to be murdered by one of his own officers. Diocletianus becomes sole ruler.

286 Diocletianus associates himself with Marcus Aurelius Valerius Maximianus, **Maximianus (Herculius)**, and the two men share imperial power.

287 Commander of the North Gallic fleet, Marcus Aurelius Mausaeus **Carausius**, declares himself Emperor in Britain. He is defeated by Maximianus, apparently in a naval engagement and is finally murdered by his chief minister, Gaius **Allectus**, in 293.

296 Flavius Valerius Constantius invades Britain for the central government and Allectus is killed in the fighting.

305 Diocletianus and Maximianus abdicate and are succeeded by Constantius, **Constantius I Chlorus**. Gaius **Galerius** Valerius Maximianus, created Caesar by Diocletianus, takes the title *Augustus* and names Flavius Valerius **Severus** as *Caesar*.

306 Flavius Valerius Aurelius **Constantinus** is proclaimed Emperor at *Eboracum* (York) on the death of his father Constantius Chlorus.

Marcus Aurelius Valerius **Maxentius** is proclaimed Emperor by the Praetorian Guard. Maxentius eliminates Severus and causes Galerius to flee from Italy.

308 Constantinus takes the title of *Augustus* in opposition to Maxentius.

312 Maxentius is defeated by Constantinus at the battle of *Pons Milvius* and Maxentius is drowned in the river Tiber in the ensuing rout. Constantinus shares power with Galerius Valerius Maximinus, **Maximinus II Daza**, and Publius Flavius Galerius Valerius Licianus Licinius, **Licinius I**.

313 Constantinus and Licinius issue the Edict of Milan, which recognises Christianity as a legal religion of the Roman Empire.

324 Licinius attempts to overthrow Constantinus, but is captured and put to death. Constantinus becomes sole ruler.

331 Constantinus moves the seat of government of the eastern Empire to Constantinople.

Introduction

To understand what manner of man the Roman soldier was, it is of foremost importance to visualise the world into which he was born and the constantly changing circumstances within that world. Any pretence that the life of ancient man was not as hard, indeed brutal, as we are often led to believe by the many cinematographic portrayals of that period of history would be a delusion; life for the vast majority of people was a continual struggle for survival, against not only natural calamity, but also the greed and savagery of their fellows.

Equally, it would be a false impression of that world to assess our ancient ancestors purely in such negative terms. To this day, we are still privileged to look upon the colossal remains of great aqueducts, which so impressed medieval man in his simplicity that he considered those huge works to have been built to supply wine to super-human Romans. Much of the

The ditch (*fossa*) on the north side of Hadrian's Wall. Great basalt boulders lie strewn on the ground where the Romans left them. Teppermoor Hill.

The ditch of Hadrian's Wall at Teppermoor Hill was never completely finished; this huge boulder was incised for splitting-wedges.

PLATE I   Caesar's army being surprised by Belgic warriors at the river Sambre, 57 BC

This plate shows the only time that Caesar was surprised by an enemy force. So sudden was the Belgic attack that the legionaries were unable to remove their shield-covers or put on their helmets. Caesar also tells us that it was normal practice to attach helmet crests and to put on *dona* (awards for bravery) when preparing for battle. The legionaries' body defences were *loricae hamatae* (mail hauberks) without sleeves, but with a mail cape similar to those of earlier Celtic hauberks. The infantry helmets shown are of Montefortino type 'C', simple bronze pieces mass-produced for the arming of soldiers who were too poor to afford more elaborate equipment. Two *pila* (javelins) were certainly carried by the legionaries in the second century BC; however, it is conceivable that by this date they were only carrying one each.

The centurion is wearing a helmet of Romano-Corinthian type, a pattern based on the Corinthian 'face' helmet, but fitted with cheek-guards by the Romans. The transverse crest is based upon sculptural evidence, but such crests were certainly worn by later centurions. He wears a short muscled cuirass, which was necessary for horsemen; the longer pattern which covered the abdomen could only be worn by a man on foot. The colour of his crest, tunic and shield indicate that he belongs to another *cohors* (cohort). The Roman historian Vegetius, though writing at a much later date, tells us that the colours were varied in this way, presumably to aid identification of units in the field.

The military tribune who has been thrown from his horse is also wearing a short cuirass with *pteruges* (strip defences) of white linen. The *pteruges* of lower-ranking soldiers were probably made from hide, for practical reasons. Tribunes were usually young men serving in the army as a step in their careers and were sometimes rather an embarrassment; when Caesar was preparing to march against the German King Ariovistus, these young men became so terrified that they tried to excuse themselves from duty and even wept openly.

Stela of the legionary Gaius Valerius Crispus of LEGIO VIII AUGUSTA, mid-second half of the first century AD. In the collection of the Städtisches Museum, Wiesbaden, Germany.

monumental road system, which, together with shipping, connected all the corners of the civilised world, may yet be found the fastest and easiest means of access to many localities.

Clearly then, there were fine architects and engineers, whose works never offended against nature, but blended with it and still do, even in ruin. Through the tireless efforts of the archaeologist, more and more of the hitherto undiscovered and long forgotten aspects of the world the Romans knew are brought before our eyes, to enchant and amaze us; or by

Hadrian's Wall at Hare Hill. This restored fragment is the highest remaining part of the Wall.

way of other better-known practices in the mighty amphitheatres, to remind us to what depths of nightmarish behaviour the human being is capable of descent.

Though so much of the immense jigsaw puzzle of that world awaits completion, it is possible to rebuild in the mind a large part of the glittering brilliance and formidable military power of Rome, which led the Roman historian Livy to observe that 'No human strength can resist Roman arms'.

For many of the warriors who nailed together the Roman Empire across

Housesteads Fort on Hadrian's Wall. This fort on the Whin Sill ridge was probably always garrisoned with infantry. In the third and fourth centuries, it was the base of the thousand-strong COHORS I TUNGRORUM. The fort also had an extensive *vicus* or civil settlement, to the south.

a thousand battlefields, enlistment in the army represented a means of livelihood little worse, and in many cases, probably better than an impoverished civilian existence, certainly in the early first century BC; rather than the heroic sacrifice of a comfortable life, for the defence of their world and the spread of enlightenment.

Be that as it may, the Roman soldier was, however unwittingly, the

 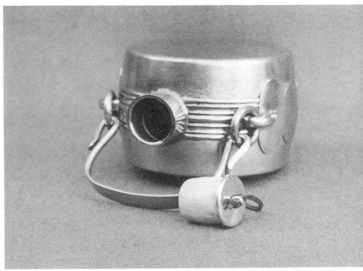

Iron field flask, made in two halves with bronze fittings; the carrying handle is presumed. Author's reconstruction based on the remains of a flask from the site of the fort of *Trimontium*, Newstead, Scotland, first century AD.

primary agent for the propagation of Roman ideas and the establishment of a settled way of life, even if it was qualified all too often by human failings. A large number of the peoples upon whom the benefits of Roman civilisation were so visited had enjoyed a life of so-called 'barbarian freedom', which, in reality, meant internecine warfare, squalid living conditions and no tangible hope of future advancement. Though the initial shock of conquest and the often unjust treatment of the subjugated nation must seem unacceptable behaviour to many people today, it is all too easy to overlook the fact that a good proportion of those brought so roughly within the Roman pale, settled down under the great *imperium* and flourished. Some became Roman citizens themselves, by military service in the auxiliary arm of Rome's forces; others by services rendered to the Empire in a variety of ways. Once gained, citizenship was hereditary and carried with it substantial benefits under the Roman system.

The reality of service life, even if it did offer certain ultimate advantages to both citizen and non-citizen, was harsh, with a rather limited chance that the individual would survive the 25 years' enlistment term, which usually began at the age of 18; many of the inscriptions upon surviving grave *stelae* indicate that the men frequently died before, or shortly after, the age of 30. Unfortunately, the cause of death is not recorded, unless the man had been killed in action, as was the case with *Centurio* Marcus Caelius, whose legion was destroyed along with two others and their auxiliaries in the Teutoburg Forest by the German chieftain Arminius in AD 9. One assumes therefore that the majority of the premature deaths were caused by disease, accidents, or possibly blood-poisoning contracted from infected wounds that could have readily been incurred in the normal course of everyday military life.

The selection of men who were fit for service in Rome's armies was carried out initially by a board of experienced officers, schooled in the

Cast of the grave *stela* of Titus Flavius Bassus, who served with the ALA NORICUM in the mid-second half of the first century AD. The original *stela* is in the collection of the Römisch-Germanisches Museum, Cologne.

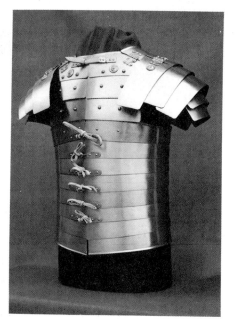

Laminated iron plate cuirass of Corbridge type 'A'. Armours of this type may have been devised to compensate for the loss of equipment suffered by the Rhine legions in AD 9. Author's reconstruction.

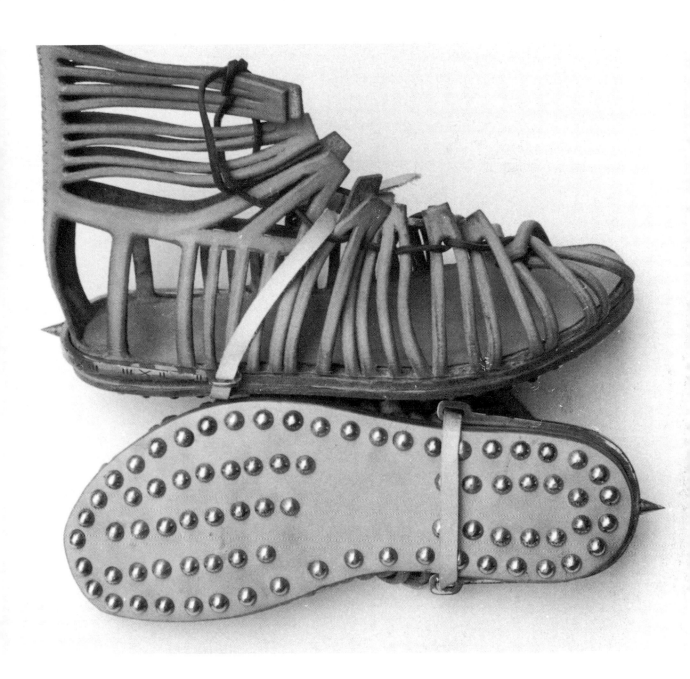

The common military boot (*caliga*), used by both infantry and cavalry. The author's reconstructions are shown with spurs, based on a specimen from Hod Hill, Dorset, England.

selection of the best fighting material. Recruits were required to be, in the words of the British Parachute Regiment recruitment pamphlet, 'of high quality, both in mind and body'.

The physical characteristics probably varied considerably from the ideal type described by the Roman historian Vegetius; 'So a young man who would be thought suitable for warfare should have shining eyes, an erect carriage, a broad chest, muscular shoulders, strong arms, long fingers, a modest belly, feet and calves sinewy...'. A height of six *pedes* (about

Section of the reliefs of Trajan's Column, Rome, showing legionary infantry and standard-bearers. Note the reduction in the size of the shields.

1.7 m or 5 ft 10 in) was considered desirable; however, since LEGIO I ITALICA, raised by the Emperor Nero in AD 67, contained men who were all of Italian origin and all of that minimum height, and that was regarded as special, other legions doubtless contained men of lesser physical stature. This belief is borne out, to an extent, by the remains of two laminated iron plate cuirasses, found at Corbridge, England, in 1964, which have a girdle length more suitable for a modern youth aged between twelve and fourteen; not the robust figure of a young man nearly six *pedes* tall, with the physique suggested by Vegetius.

It should be noted, however, that there is now some reason to believe that the laminated iron cuirass (*lorica segmentata*), was not confined to use by legionary infantrymen, but was most probably in quite common usage in the *cohortes* of auxiliary infantry. Certainly the stature of auxiliaries serving with the cavalry *alae* and *cohortes equitatae* was sometimes quite small; the remains of an iron cavalry helmet of first-century AD date, found on the site of the fort of *Trimontium*, Newstead, Scotland, is of such small dimensions that it must have belonged to a man of no more than five and a half *pedes*.

The accepted applicant then passed into a period called *probatio*, which again has its modern parallel, during which he underwent a more

26

Left:
South gateway of Cawfields milecastle on Hadrian's Wall. Note the recesses for the timber gates.

Right:
Cawfields milecastle on Hadrian's Wall.

thorough medical examination. Those found to have physical defects which were not immediately obvious to the selection board were discharged; one may expect that weak eyesight was a common cause of failure. *Probatio* was probably also used to scrutinise the character of the applicant; for laziness, immorality and dishonesty were unwelcome blemishes in a force where discipline was vital to the well-being of all. Occasionally, men did fall from grace, to be rewarded with a variety of punishments, up to and including the death penalty.

Capital punishment was probably fairly infrequent and applied only to the more serious offences of mutiny, cowardice and the sometimes understandable fault of falling asleep on sentry duty. To be caught 'napping' after a gruelling march and to be executed for it might appear somewhat extreme to many; however, the Roman military took the matter very seriously, for the man who neglected his duty in that way endangered not only himself but also his comrades and it was his own section which carried out sentence.

Recruits were then posted to special training camps, where all the basics, such as entrenching, rampart construction and, naturally, weapons and marching drill, were taught. Apparently, Roman infantry also had to have some knowledge of handling army animals and some instruction in riding was also included in the programme. Training certainly did not cease upon leaving such camps; indeed the constant army manoeuvres, undertaken

27

with great realism, caused the Jewish historian Flavius Josephus to write in his brief description of the Roman military, 'It would not be far from the truth to call their drills bloodless battles, their battles bloody drills'. And so the Romans were always in a constant state of readiness for war.

Men who took the trouble to obtain special proficiencies, perhaps as masons or metal-workers, could attain the rank of *immunis* which meant not only a higher rate of pay, but also immunity from the more disagreeable tasks, which were no less necessary in ancient times than they have been ever since. Another, though rather dubious, method of avoiding such fatigues, was the practice of bribery of the centurionate.

Weapon training was most important. The intelligent use of the sword is mentioned particularly in a surviving Roman training manual. The method taught was to thrust, rather than to slash at an opponent; for a slash-cut rarely kills, but a thrust makes a deep penetration of the vital organs. The Roman short sword was clearly designed for stabbing, with its sharp angled point, though it could be, and certainly was on occasion, used to effect cutting strokes. The skulls belonging to the hapless defenders of the great Durotrigian fortress of Maiden Castle in Dorset, England, show the appalling fatal wounds inflicted by the soldiers of LEGIO II AUGUSTA against adversaries who were most probably unhelmeted.

Remains of a turret on Hadrian's Wall at Brunton, near Chollerford. The position of the doorway (to the right) indicates that it may have been the work of LEGIO XX VALERIA VICTRIX.

28

Leather satchel, which probably held personal effects; a mess-tin (*patera*); and a camp kettle.

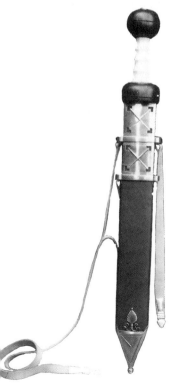

Sword and scabbard with mounts of simple type, from Long Windsor, Dorset, England. The blade form was the same as the Pompeii type overleaf. Author's reconstruction.

The use of the thrust also meant that the Roman kept himself covered with the bones of his own arm. To raise the arm to make a cut necessarily exposed his entire right side; this fact was to be exploited by the Hanoverian force, under the command of William, Duke of Cumberland, on sorrowful Drummossie Muir in 1746 against the Jacobite rebels. Wielding their broadswords above their heads, the Highlanders fell victim to the long wicked bayonets of the infantry, who were instructed to direct their thrusts to the right, instead of at the man in front.

The diet of the Roman soldier was long believed to have been vegetarian; a belief supported by an observation made by the Roman historian Tacitus, who, in describing the siege of *Tigranocerta*, stated that the Romans ate meat only when threatened with starvation. It is impossible to reconcile Tacitus' observation with current archaeological knowledge, which shows conclusively that meat was consumed in the forts, along with a great variety of other foodstuffs.

It is reasonable to believe that the troops were supplied with non-perishable rations in the field; such comestibles as cheese, bacon and grain could be carried for several days without fear of contamination and it may be that flesh was avoided for that reason, which led Tacitus to make such an apparently misleading statement. Ancient health laws governing the eating of meat are still to be found today, under the guise of religious belief.

Grain was a substantial part of the campaign rations and soldiers with sickles may be seen harvesting wheat in one of the multifarious scenes of military life portrayed on Trajan's Column in Rome, an immense sculptural work erected in the early second century AD which com-memorates that Emperor's victories over the Dacians. To process the grain

29

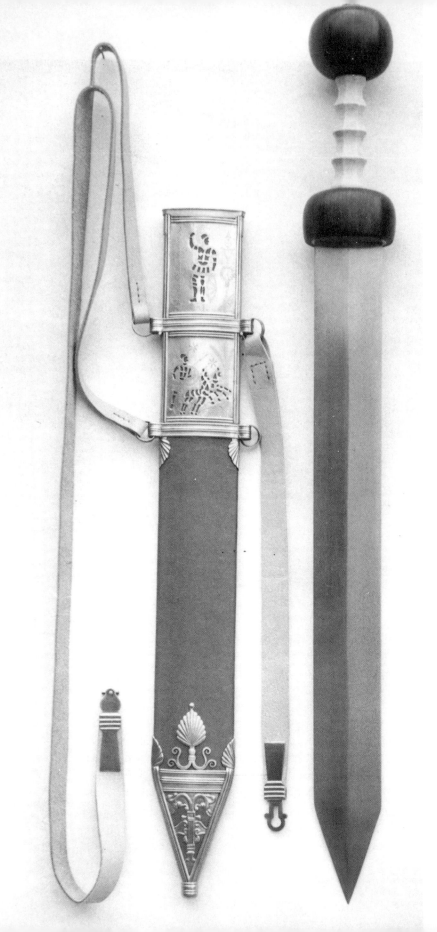

Sword and scabbard of Pompeii pattern. Introduced in the early first century AD, the pattern ran concurrently with older types for many years. Author's reconstruction.

Corbridge (*Corstopitum*), supply depôt for Hadrian's Wall. One of two large stone granaries (*horrea*).

for consumption, the soldiers carried small stone querns, which were probably transported by the baggage train in carts, because of their weight. A quern of this type was reconstructed for the trans-Alpine march undertaken by Dr Marcus Junkelmann, MA, as part of the celebrations of the founding of the city of Augsburg in 15 BC. The manually operated quern was found to be quite satisfactory and the resultant flour could be used in a number of ways, which could be employed to make the field rations somewhat less monotonous; for example, a dough was made with honey, the Roman source of sugar, and then baked on hot stones surrounding camp fires.

Army pay, no matter how much the soldiers may have grumbled, seems to have been reasonably adequate. Upon joining a unit, a recruit was presumably issued with a complete set of equipment, which it is thought he had to purchase from the State by regular deductions, added to which were stoppages for bedding, food, boots and straps, clothing, the annual camp dinner (presumably the legion's birthday), and a burial premium. Part of the remaining income of the men was retained and deposited in the

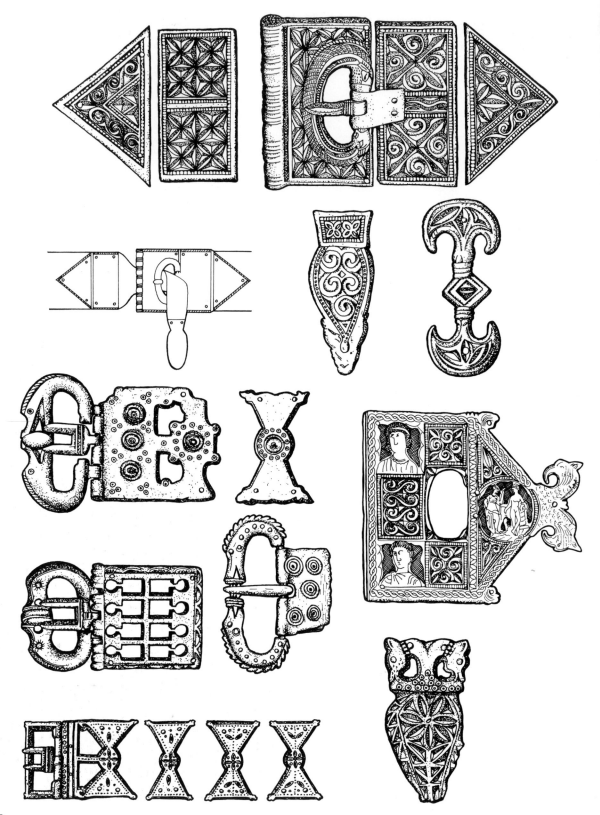

Opposite:
Bronze military belt fittings of the fourth to fifth century. Many such fittings were 'chip' carved to produce intricate patterns.

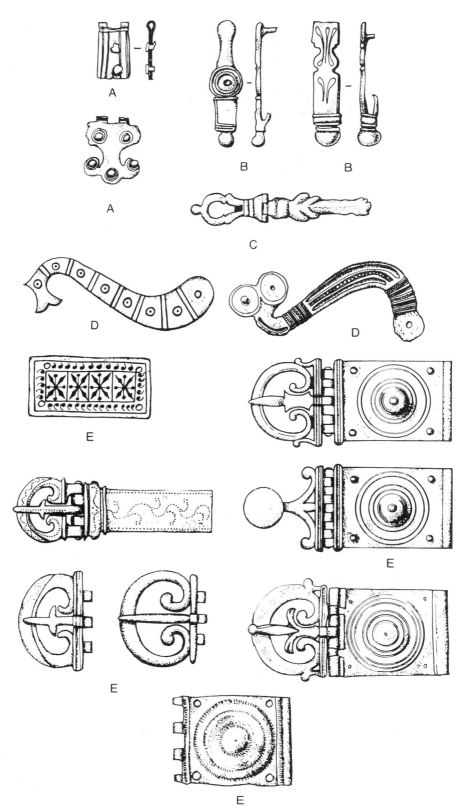

Tinned or silvered military artefacts of bronze.
A   fittings from a *lorica segmentata*, plain bronze
B   cavalry harness decorations
C   baldric fastener, or harness attachment
D   hauberk breast-hooks
E   belt fittings

33

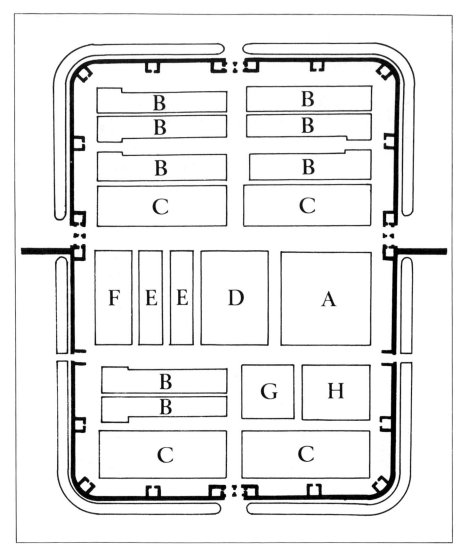

Plan of the Chesters Fort on
Hadrian's Wall.
A   commander's quarters
B   barracks
C   stabling
D   headquarters
E   granaries
F   workshop
G   stores?
H   hospital

army bank, in order that they would not squander their entire pay and
bonuses. Even after all those deductions, the men apparently had money
enough to indulge in gambling; a favourite pursuit, normally carried out
during the periods of relaxation in the fort bath-house.

The bath-houses provided the men with the Roman equivalent of a
Turkish bath, in the form of three rooms of varying temperature: *tepid-
arium*, *calidarium* and *frigidarium*, warm, hot and cold. The heating was
supplied by a furnace and a large hot-water tank, the residual heat from
the furnace being used to supply a hot dry room, by means of the familiar
Roman hypocaust or under-floor system.

A very fine and well-preserved example of such an establishment is to
be found attached to the Chesters Fort, Roman *Cilurnum*, on Hadrian's
Wall, England. There is also a latrine in the bath-house block, the outflow
discharging into the North Tyne river close by. One may imagine that such

Plan of a military bath-house
(Chesters).
A   changing room
B   hot room
C   hot bath
D   hot room
E   boiler
F   warm rooms
G   cold room
g   cold plunge
H   cold bath
J   latrine
K   sewage outflow
S   stoke-holes

34

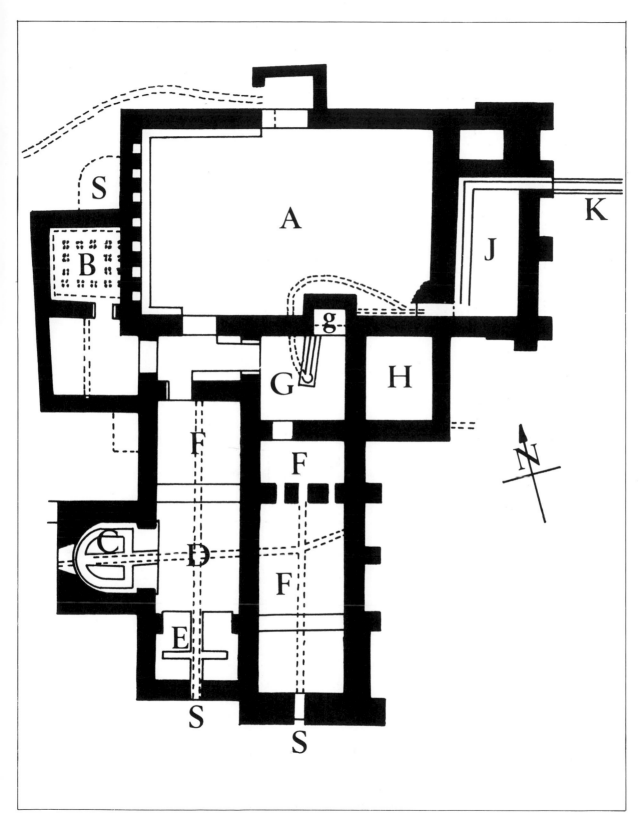

Changing and recreation room of the bath-house of the Chesters Fort on Hadrian's Wall. The purpose of the niches is uncertain, but they may have held bathers' clothing.

Stonework of the bridge abutment near the Chesters Fort, where the Wall crossed the North Tyne river. Good-quality masonry was clearly necessary for such structures.

bathing establishments were especially well frequented during the long bitter winters which are to be encountered in northern Britain; men posted from countries in the eastern Mediterranean must have been heartily relieved to be returned to warmer climatic conditions.

All things considered, the Roman State took good care of its servicemen and the individual could look forward to a reasonably secure future upon retirement. Though in common with all soldiers before and since, they occasionally suffered from incompetent generalship, political upheavals and latterly inferior arms in face of the overwhelming military capability of other nations, the Roman will always be revered as the first truly professional warrior of all time, to stand proudly in the annals of military history.

Gaius Marius and Gaius Julius Caesar

c. 157–86 BC *c.* 100–44 BC

Gaius Marius, who is regarded by many as the innovator who changed the old armies of the Roman Republic into the splendid fighting machine of popular legend, was a man of relatively humble origins, certainly in the eyes of the ruling Patrician class, born the son of a farmer at *Arpinum*, 96 km (60 mi) east of the City of Rome.

The young Marius was a tough and quite ruthless character, with few, if any, illusions about the Roman State and its government. Though not a brilliant orator or politician of the upper-class mould, he gained the support of the common people as a champion of their rights and successfully asserted himself into the political arena, despite the disadvantage

PLATE 2   The aftermath of a battle in southern Gaul, AD 22. A Gallic revolt has been suppressed by LEGIO II AUGUSTA

The equipment of the legionary infantryman is typical of the late Augustan to early Tiberian period. His *lorica hamata* is fitted with a shoulder-doubling of Greek outline, fastened at the breast with hooks which prevented the doubling from slipping outwards. This form of doubling appears to have been the type worn exclusively by the infantry. The main body of the hauberk has been worked to cover the deltoids, which may indicate the use of simple expansions in the construction of the mail; however, there is yet no surviving fragment of Roman mail which shows such knowledge in mail-making tehnique. The *pteruges* at the upper arms would have been attached to an arming-doublet worn beneath the main corselet of mail. Such doublets were probably the sole method used for the suspension of all defences of *pteruges*, either of linen or leather. The hauberk is secured at the waist with a pair of belts which carry the sidearms. During the first half of the first

century AD, a groin-guard was introduced; initially it consisted of the strap-end of one belt cut into four narrow strips, one of which passed through the buckle, and all four were provided with small metal terminals. The groin-guard later became a much more elaborate item of equipment, especially those of the auxiliary infantry shown on grave *stelae* of the mid first century. The helmet is of Coolus type 'D', based on a specimen from Haltern, now in the Münster Museum. These helmets often carried side plumes as well as a hair crest. The shield is the second stage in the development of the *scutum*. The top and bottom curves have been removed, leaving the curved sides. The central rib or 'spine' on the early *scutum* has also disappeared and it is thought that the shield-board had been reduced in thickness and fitted with back-bracing to compensate for the loss of rigidity.

One of the figures of Roman cavalrymen portrayed in the battle-reliefs on the Arch of Orange,

which commemorates the suppression of the revolt, is shown to wear a helmet of Coolus type, like that depicted in the illustration. Helmets of this kind were probably issued to the auxiliary cavalry in the absence of any properly designed head-pieces for cavalry use. It is most likely that such helmets as the Weiler type were already in production, but time in manufacture would have meant very slow distribution. The figure wears a short *lorica hamata*, slit at the sides to facilitate sitting a mount. The straps of the shoulder-doubling were rather small and of the Greek type; the Celtic 'cape' doubling seems to have totally superseded the Greek pattern by the second half of the century. The cavalry figures of the Arch of Orange are not shown to wear *feminalia* (knee-breeches); however, the wearing of such clothing could depend upon climatic conditions. The cavalry wore the same *caligae* (military boots) as the infantry, but fitted with spurs.

of being what the Patricians derisively called 'a new man', one who had no Consuls among his ancestors. Anxious to make good that lack of social standing, he married into the powerful clan of the Julii; incidentally becoming in the process the uncle of Rome's most famous soldier, his wife's nephew Gaius Julius Caesar.

An opportunity to gain military distinction, always a helpful step for an ambitious individual under the Roman system, came with the outbreak of a minor war in North Africa, within the client kingdom of *Numidia*. On the death of Micipsa, the King of *Numidia*, in 188 BC, the country was to be ruled by the King's own two sons, Adherbal and Hiempsal, and his nephew Jugurtha, whom he had adopted upon receiving a most laudatory report of the young man's conduct from the Roman general Publius Scipio, concerning his services during the siege of *Numantia* in Spain. Fine soldier though he undoubtedly was, Jugurtha was also shrewd, cunning and probably even more ruthless than Gaius Marius, when it came to his own advancement.

After much intrigue, Jugurtha succeeded in eliminating both of Micipsa's sons, but also made the mistake of dispatching a number of Italian traders after the surrender of the Numidian town of *Cirta*, where Adherbal had sought sanctuary, in 112.

War was declared and the following year the Roman Senate duly appointed the Consul Lucius Calpurnius Bestia to take command of an army.

Unfortunately for the Roman cause, Bestia, it transpired, was a very poor choice of commander, for he was more interested in what he could gain for himself in the way of personal wealth, than in carrying out his mission. So it became a matter of ease for Jugurtha to simply bribe Bestia into inactivity and make mock submission to the will of Rome.

Further campaigns by Spurius Postumius Albinus and his brother Aulus in 110 proved equally fruitless and it was not until the appointment of Quintus Caecilius Metellus to the command over the next two years that any real headway was made against Jugurtha. However, the war was taking place in a region where Jugurtha could call upon many allies, or escape capture with a facility which made the termination of the war seem impossible under the direction of Metellus.

At least, that was how Gaius Marius, who was serving under Metellus, made the difficulties appear to the Roman public, and by such methods he had himself elected Consul for the year 107 and deprived Metellus of the command in *Numidia*, taking over the post himself.

Despite successful operations by Marius in 107 and 106, Jugurtha continued to elude capture and it was not until 105 that he was finally taken, and then only as a result of treachery on the part of one of his allies. The man who actually set the trap for Jugurtha was Marius's subordinate, Lucius Cornelius Sulla, a man who was later to be the downfall of Marius.

During the Marian campaigns in *Numidia*, far more serious trouble was brewing north of the Alps. Two large tribes, of Germanic origin, had invaded Gaul, despite the attempts by several Roman armies to halt their progress, culminating in a massive defeat at Orange (*Arausio*), where 80,000 Romans were reported to have been slain. The defeat is believed to have been inflicted by the tribe of the Cimbri alone. Instead of turning east into northern Italy, the Germans moved south into Spain and remained in that vicinity for the following three years. Italy had been spared what would no doubt have been a major disaster, as great as that suffered at the hands of the Gauls, when they invaded Italy *c.* 390 BC and briefly occupied the City of Rome.

The years of respite were not wasted and by time the Germans moved north again, Marius was waiting for them. The tribe of the Teutones were the first to taste defeat; in a bloody action at *Aquae Sextiae* (Aix-en-Provence), Marius cunningly concealed a large number of troops on high ground and once the Teutones had advanced towards his main force, suddenly attacked them in the rear. It was said that some 200,000 Germans fell in the battle and that many more were captured.

The Cimbri succeeded in penetrating northern Italy, crossed the river Po and met the Roman army at *Vercellae*, 64 km (40 mi) north-east of modern Turin. The Cimbri, abiding by what would seem a foolish custom, gave Marius the choice of ground for the battle, which he duly selected as the Raudine plain; a place which was wide and level, advantageous to his superior cavalry force. On the morning of 30 July 101, using the heavy mists to cover their movements, the Roman cavalry attacked that of the Cimbri, throwing them back in confusion onto their own infantry, as the latter were taking up their battle positions. Wholesale slaughter ensued and the Cimbri were annihilated; other tribesmen who had followed them in the hopes of entering Italy after the Romans had been defeated, turned back and fled northward.

Marius was at the height of his prestige, but with the Germanic threat removed, the Romans settled down to internal strife, until the ambitions of Mithridates, King of *Pontus* on the Black Sea, led him to invade the Roman client kingdom of *Bithynia* (88). Instead of calling upon Marius, whose past services seem to have faded from the Roman mind, the Senate gave the command against Mithridates to his old army subordinate, Sulla. Aided by the tribune Sulpicius Rufus, Marius managed to have Sulla's appointment quashed officially, but Sulla refused to accept the ignominy and for the first time in history, Roman troops marched against the City of Rome in defiance of the government. Rufus was caught by Sulla's supporters and put to death; Marius was more fortunate and escaped to North Africa, though in a legal state of outlawry.

No sooner had Sulla left Rome to take up the command in the East, than his political opponents seized power in Rome, in particular one Lucius Cornelius Cinna, and Marius returned from exile. Once he had mockingly had his state of outlawry reversed, Marius set about the murder of all Sulla's suporters, and for five days and nights the slaughter continued unabated in the City. The number of dead is unknown, for the campaign of terror spread throughout Italy for months; however, Marius doubtless took thorough reprisals against the nobility, who had so scornfully treated him during his life. The terror would probably have spread even further afield had not Marius died on 13 January 86 BC; one may expect that many people slept more soundly for the passing of the man who had once been the saviour of the Roman world.

For Caesar, the death of Marius signalled extreme peril, for Sulla, having forced Mithridates to come to terms, was now ready to return to Italy. The only obstacle to Sulla's hopes was Lucius Cornelius Cinna, the colleague and supporter of Marius, who began raising a force to oppose Sulla when he landed in Italy. As fortune would have it, a riot broke out in Cinna's camp and he was killed.

With Cinna conveniently removed from the scene, nothing now stood between Sulla and his desire to eliminate the 'popular' party of Marius. Caesar, though of Patrician class, was not only the nephew of Marius, but had also married the daughter of Lucius Cinna. Both ties were regarded with suspicion by Sulla and he ordered a show of loyalty to the new regime, by demanding that Caesar divorce his wife Cornelia. Caesar refused to comply and, instead, vanished into the countryside near to Rome and fell gravely ill. He was taken back to the City and nursed back to health, but he was still a marked man in the eyes of Sulla and it was only the eloquent pleas of his friends which caused Sulla to relent, with the famous remark, 'But remember. . .one Caesar is worse than a dozen Mariuses'.

With the ground in Rome so uncertain, Caesar thought it wise to leave the City for some time and took up an appointment in the eastern provinces in 81 BC. A succession of posts followed and his political influence increased by association with the immensely wealthy Marcus Licinius Crassus and Gnaeus Pompeius (Pompey the Great); the three men formed the First Triumvirate, an alliance of sufficient influence to oppose all others, though informal legally. With this backing, Caesar secured the consulship for the year 59 BC and the governorship of Illyricum and the provinces of Cisalpine Gaul (northern Italy) and the Transalpine Province.

Rome had held territory in southern Gaul since the second century BC and had established friendly, or at least peaceful, relations with some of the Gallic tribes, particularly the Aedui, whose lands lay immediately to the north of the Roman Province. There can be little doubt that Caesar saw the Province as a good starting point for further expansion in Gaul and his own personal advancement. Accordingly, he began raising troops in Cisalpine Gaul.

By April of 58 BC, disturbing reports began to reach Rome of a massive tribal migration, which apparently posed a threat to both the Roman Province and the recently subdued tribe of the Allobroges.

The migrating tribe, called the Helvetii, were of Germanic stock, though referred to as Gauls by Caesar, had become dissatisfied with their rather bleak country east of the Jura mountains (Switzerland) and had decided to move westwards to the more fertile territory of the Santoni to the north of the Pyrenees. Initially, the Helvetii proposed to cross the river Rhône near Geneva and make their way through the lands of the Allobroges, who they considered would not oppose their advance, or could be intimidated into allowing their passage. They then intended to continue their westward movement through the Roman Province and with an army of fierce warriors, said to number some 100,000 strong, the Helvetii were not concerned that any Roman objections might be expressed by force of arms.

Caesar, though taken by surprise by these events, ordered the single legion stationed in Gaul and a force of auxiliaries, hastily raised in the Province, to march north and prevent the Helvetii from crossing the Rhône. This was accomplished with considerable ease; Caesar simply constructed fortifications at the intended crossing point and demolished the only bridge over the river. Realising his serious weakness in numbers, he returned to northern Italy and enrolled two new legions, which he added to three raised previously that were in camp at *Aquileia* (near modern Monfalcone). Taking all five legions, he marched back as rapidly as possible to the Province.

Map of Gaul, 58 BC.

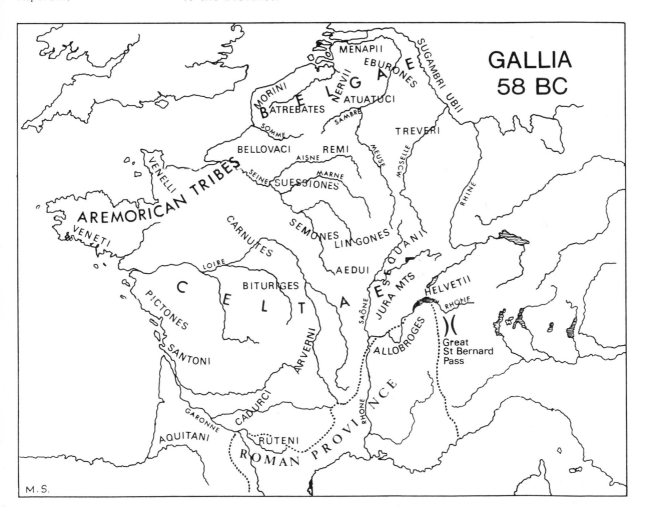

Undeterred from their migratory purpose, the Helvetii sought to change the route of their passage and enlisted the aid of a sympathetic, treacherous Aeduan chieftain, named Dumnorix, who was on friendly terms with the Sequani, through whose territory the Helvetii now proposed to journey, skirting the northern border of the Roman Province.

The acquiescence of the Sequani having been thus obtained, the Helvetii had already traversed their country and were in the process of crossing the river Saône by the time Caesar reached the northern border of the Province and entered the territory of the Segusiavi immediately beyond the Roman pale, where he encamped. Reports were brought to him from the Aedui and others that the Helvetii who had already crossed the Saône were despoiling their lands and they appealed to Caesar for help against them.

Seeing that the main part of the Helvetian force, which was on the west side of the Saône, would be unable to assist the smaller body of their army, which was not yet across the river, Caesar decided to attack at once. Taking with him three legions, marching by night, he succeeded in launching a surprise assault, killing many of those on the east side of the river and capturing their baggage; the survivors fled to the safety of the surrounding woodland.

Caesar promptly set his legionary engineers to work and threw a bridge over the Saône in one day. With the Roman army across the Saône and being greatly impressed by the speed of that accomplishment, the Helvetii attempted to sue for peace, but chose to follow up their supplication with

PLATE 3 LEGIO II AUGUSTA assaults the Durotrigian fortress of Mai-dun (Maiden Castle), Dorset, England, AD 43

The legionary infantryman is wearing a laminated iron plate cuirass of Corbridge type 'B', considered by the author to have been in circulation prior to the invasion of Britain. Armours of this type may have been designed as a means of replacing serious losses of mail hauberks on the Rhine frontier in AD 9. This cuirass differs from the earlier 'A' type (see author's reconstruction, p. 24) in two noticeable ways; the number of girdle plates has been reduced from eight to seven and the strap connections between the collar and the girdles of 'A' type have been replaced with stronger hook and loop fittings. It is thought that these body defences were probably also issued to cohortes of auxiliary infantry. The notable deficiencies of these cuirasses, which have been named loricae segmentatae in modern times, were the loss of protection to the thighs and, to an extent, the upper arms. Many of these armours were roughly made and the quite intricate hinges and buckles frequently broke, providing the legionary armourers with a constant round of repairs. Badly made collars could prove most uncomfortable and that feature may have been the reason for the introduction of the military scarf, focale. The helmet is of Imperial Gallic type 'F', based on the remains of a skull-piece found in the river Rhine at Mainz. The cheek-guards are based on the basic pattern of a specimen from the fort at Hod Hill, close to Maiden Castle. The scutum is shown in its final form, having lost its curved sides and being semi-cylindrical in appearance. It is possible that some of these shields, as also those of the cavalry, carried decoration on the face executed in light metal; however, from the available evidence, the practice appears to have been limited.

The cavalryman is wearing a body defence clearly depicted on a relief from Arlon on the Belgium−Luxembourg border. The main part of the defence is mail, but it is fitted with laminated plate shoulder-guards similar in appearance to those of the Corbridge loricae segmentatae; presumably the plates were leathered and attached in a similar fashion to those of the infantry patterns. The helmet is of Auxiliary Cavalry type 'A', found at Weiler in Luxembourg. This helmet is probably the earliest true Roman cavalry field head-piece and has a 3 mm-thick skull, giving the helmet a very long life, besides a good defensive quality.

threats. Despite being offered reasonable terms by Caesar, they continued in their arrogance and the chance for a bloodless solution was lost.

Considering that the Helvetian force was too large to engage in a major battle without advantageous ground, Caesar chose to shadow them at some miles distant, but close enough to prevent the enemy from scattering their forces in pursuit of plunder. Soon, however, his food supplies began to run dangerously low, since supplies which had been promised by the Aedui had failed to arrive. At that point the treachery of some of the Aeduans surfaced, especially that of Dumnorix, whose secret dealings with the Helvetii, Caesar was informed, were the true cause of the delay in the supply of provisions. Wisely, because of the popularity of Dumnorix and the consequent enmity his execution would have caused among the Gauls, Caesar simply warned Dumnorix against further activities of the kind, but at the same time had him watched in order to discover the identity of any others who were in sympathy with the anti-Roman faction.

No sooner was that matter concluded, than news reached Caesar that the Helvetii had halted near to a hill about 12.8 km (8 mi) from the Roman force. Caesar decided to engage them at that place. Unbelievably, he was given a completely inaccurate report concerning the enemy's disposition by a member of his own staff and was forced to adandon his plan. Now that his army was approaching total exhaustion of rations, he ordered the whole force to march towards the Aeduan capital of *Bibracte* (near modern Autun), where they would be able to obtain fresh supplies.

The Helvetii, upon receiving news of the Roman direction of march, considered that Caesar had ordered a retreat and set off in pursuit, making harassing moves against the Roman rearguard. The Helvetians' assumption proved to be their undoing, for now Caesar had made his sorely-needed choice of ground and turned to give battle. The site he selected was a small hill, and he stationed his veteran legionaries in three lines on the forward slope; all his more recently raised legionaries and the auxiliary force were positioned at the summit.

The Roman cavalry force, which was largely comprised of Aeduan Gauls, attempted to engage the enemy, but were easily brushed aside and the Helvetii advanced against the waiting Roman infantry in a dense phalanx formation. Caesar clearly thought the battle was going to be a hard-fought one, for he sent all horses away out of reach, so that none could take flight with any ease.

The ensuing battle was far easier at the outset than the Romans had expected. The phalanx of the enemy presented a huge target into which they rained javelins and spears, killing and wounding many. Once the close combat was joined, the Romans found the Helvetians no match for them and drove them back to another hill 1.6 km (1 mi) distant from their own position. There the Helvetii managed to gain the high ground and the impetus of the Roman legionaries was lost. As the Romans prepared to drive the enemy from their position, the Helvetian rearguard, who had taken no part in the action up to that time, suddenly appeared on the

Roman right flank and opened a second front. Heartened by the sight of their comrades, the force on the hill renewed their efforts, obliging the Romans to divide their force, in order to fight on both fronts at the same time.

The fighting continued from midday until late at night, but at length Roman military prowess prevailed against the desperate bravery of their adversaries. Some of the Helvetii surrendered, others fled northward towards the territory of the Lingones, hoping to escape Roman pursuit. Caesar, however, sent instructions to the Lingones that no aid or succour of any kind was to be extended to the fugitives, or he would regard such an action as hostile and treat them accordingly. After three days, during which time the battlefield was cleared and the wounded given medical attention, Caesar set off to recapture the Helvetians. Even as he was on the march, envoys came to him beseeching him to allow peaceful surrender. But some six thousand of the Helvetians thought they might be able to escape across the river Rhine and made away under cover of night. Caesar was informed of their attempt and caused them to be returned, whereupon he had them all executed. The remainder were allowed to surrender as they had requested and Caesar ordered them to return whence they came. So great had been the loss of life, that of the 368,000 men, women and children who had begun the trek westwards, only 110,000 ever returned home again.

Shortly after the Helvetii were vanquished, another problem was brought before Caesar by the Gauls. During the early 60s BC, the tribe of Sequani had hired some 15,000 German warriors to aid them in an inter-tribal struggle with their neighbours in central Gaul, who were under the domination of the Aedui. Once the Sequani had triumphed over their enemies, they found themselves unwilling hosts to the Germans, who had decided that they had no wish to return to their homelands. Instead they were joined by another 24,000 of the tribe of the Harudes. The Gauls, who had already lost a third of their lands to their mercenaries, were bluntly told by the German King, Ariovistus, that they were now to hand over another third.

It was clear to all the Gauls that such appropriation of their lands would not stop at that and so they appealed to Caesar once more for Roman assistance. Caesar, of course, recognised that the Germans were a threat to Roman interests, quite as much as to the Gauls. Envoys duly passed between Caesar and the German King, the relations growing more strained at each attempt by Caesar to curb Ariovistus' ambitions in Gaul. Finally, the German told Caesar quite bluntly to stay out of their affairs or it would be the worse for the Romans.

Further reports reached Caesar that more Germans were about to cross the Rhine and he decided upon immediate intervention, for fear that the numbers already under the command of Ariovistus should be increased to a point where they would be uncontrollable.

Whilst on the march, he learned that the Germans were making for the

Sequanian town of *Vesontio* (Besançon), where it was known that considerable supplies would fall into their hands, unless they were checked.

Accordingly, Caesar advanced to the town by forced march, day and night, and occupied it. In the days that followed, while Caesar was provisioning his army, the local Gauls propagated stories of the great stature and ferocious bearing of the German warriors and had so affrighted many of the young, inexperienced officers, that they began to find urgent reasons for not being there, or even wept openly and generally behaved as if their lives were already lost. The fear proved infectious and eventually Caesar was told that the force would refuse to march against Ariovistus when the order was given.

Caesar called all the centurions to a council and led them to believe that Ariovistus was not really disposed to make war upon them; but even if he did, there was no cause for alarm. He cited many instances of German defeats by the Romans, even by the Helvetii, so recently beaten by themselves. The Germans, in his opinion, could only hope to win by trickery, and that only when fighting simple natives. So finally, Caesar said that he proposed to test the loyalty of his troops, he would move his camp towards Ariovistus in the early hours of the morning, taking with him LEGIO X if no other would join him. On hearing the words of their com-

PLATE 4   Two cavalry troopers of the ALA NORICUM in battle order passing a fort's timber granary, based on the reconstructed granary at the Lunt Fort Interpretive Centre, Coventry, England. Mid-second half of the first century AD

The trooper wearing a helmet of Weiler type, as shown in Plate 3, is based on the grave *stela* of Titus Flavius Bassus from Cologne, in the collection of the Römisch–Germanisches Museum, Cologne. Though head-pieces of this type were made in the early part of the century, they clearly were still in service as late as the date of these troopers. Though sculptors usually represented the early cavalry helmets with vertical brow plates, the treatment of the hair on the *stela* of Bassus bears a marked resemblance to the Weiler helmet and a fragment of an identical helmet found on the site of the fortress at Longthorpe, near Peterborough, England, which dates from the time of the Boudican Revolt. Since the ALA NORICUM does not appear to have served in Britain, it is clear that similar helmets were to be found in other cavalry regiments. He wears a *lorica hamata* with a shoulder-doubling cape of mail, which had become the norm

for cavalrymen by this date, though it appears that some body defences were no longer fitted with a doubling of any kind. The scabbard of his *spatha* is mounted with separate locket and chape metals. The sculptural respresentations of all scabbards appear to show the continued use of side-gutters; however, this probably owes to the common habit of 'stiffening' the appearance of some objects in reliefs by cutting lines along edges where, in fact, they did not exist. This sculptor's technique may also be seen applied to many of the *loricae segmentatae* portrayed on Trajan's Column.

The second trooper is based on the *stela* of Gaius Romanius in the collection of the Mittelrheinisches Landesmuseum, Mainz. The helmet shown on the *stela* has embossed hair very similar in treatment to the helmet skull-piece found at Northwich, Cheshire, England. However, the oddly high-angled brow edge of the Northwich piece is

not shown and is replaced with a vertical brow-plate, similar to Bassus'. The body defence is a *lorica squamata* of relatively large scales, an example of which was also found on the site of the Longthorpe fortress. Neither of these *stelae* shows any detail of the defensive material from which the body armours were made; they were most probably represented in paint.

The pony's saddle carries a quiver for light javelins as described by the Jewish historian Josephus in *The Jewish War*. The only other evidence for the existence of such quivers is an object of this appearance being carried by a *calo* (attendant or servant) on the *stela* of a cavalryman in Germany. The use of light javelins, however, does bear a close relation to the cavalry 'game', the *hippika gymnasia*, in which the contestants threw light dummy javelins at each other: the game may well have been a display of actual battle prowess.

mander, the men's fears simply evaporated and when, as he had said, Caesar marched out in the early hours, all his troops marched with him.

When Ariovistus was apprised of Caesar's march towards him, he sent word that he would now be willing to hold a conference, which he had previously refused to do, and a meeting was duly arranged. However, attempts by Caesar to come to terms with the German King proved fruitless and the conference was called off when the German bodyguard started to attack Caesar's mounted legionaries.

Ariovistus made the next move, by marching his army past the Roman encampment and placing his force in a position where he could cut Caesar's lines of supply. The manoeuvre was regarded as most serious by the Romans, freshly provisioned though they were, and Caesar made repeated attempts to provoke the Germans into an engagement, but they refused to be drawn. Interrogation of German prisoners revealed the reason. The customary divination, practised by all ancients, had indicated that if Ariovistus joined battle before the new moon appeared, he would be defeated.

The information was a considerable stroke of good fortune for Caesar and he moved his six legions right up to the Germans' encampment, forcing them to accept battle. They thereupon emerged from their camp and took up their battle positions by tribes, parking all their wheeled transport to their rear, so that there would be no retreat. They placed their womenfolk in the wagons, so that they could implore their men not to let them fall into Roman slavery, as they marched to the battle lines; an obvious indication that, despite their numerical superiority, the Germans were doubtful of the outcome.

Caesar began the battle by leading his right wing against the German left, which he had noticed was the weakest part of their line, and broke them. The left of the Roman line was not so favoured by the Gods; the large numbers of Germans were pressing back the legionaries and their position was becoming very dangerous. Caesar himself, being in the midst of the fighting on the right, could not see the peril and give orders accordingly; but a young cavalry officer saved the day by calling up the reserve third line. The fresh troops turned the tide of battle and the Germans were forced to turn tail and make for the Rhine. The Roman cavalry, as usual, went in pursuit and killed all they could find. A very few managed to escape across the river, including Ariovistus, who was fortunate enough to find a boat.

With winter coming on, Caesar quartered his army in the territory of the Sequani and returned to Italy. During the winter, intelligence reports reached him that the Belgic tribes of northern Gaul were making military preparations, no doubt fearing that the Roman army that had remained in Gaul would, sooner or later, be used against them. Caesar began to make plans to crush any warlike intentions on the part of the Belgae, which might encourage other tribes, already subdued, to rise against the Romans. He raised two more legions and sent them to Gaul as soon as the spring weather arrived, following on in person once the food supply situation permitted the start of a campaign.

In two weeks, Caesar had moved his army north and had entered the lands of the Remi, who placed themselves under his protection and promised aid. Upon learning that the hostile force of Belgae were on the move, Caesar crossed the river Aisne into their territory. The two armies encamped about 3 km (2 mi) apart and from the extent of the enemy watchfires, it was clear to Caesar that their strength was very great.

By skirmishing, Caesar learned that the quality of the enemy troops was not as high as he had been led to believe and decided upon a major engagement. He marshalled his legions in front of his camp and had deep ditches dug along both flanks at right angles to the front, protected at both ends by *catapultae*. By this means, he presented a short front as a counter to his enemies' superior numbers; much as Suetonius Paullinus was to do a hundred years later against Queen Boudica in Britain.

The Belgae refused the battle offered to them and instead put some troops across the river and tried to cut the Roman lines of communication. Caesar forthwith led a force of cavalry, archers, slingers and light-armed Numidians back across the Aisne and in the action that followed killed a large number of the Belgae, mostly in the river.

The defeat was severe enough to break the will of the Belgae to attempt a further confrontation and they decided to return to their homes and wait upon events. As the tribesmen left their camp amidst much noise and confusion during the night, Caesar made no move to pursue them, fearing that he might be ambushed; but by the morning it was clear that the Belgae had genuinely retreated. The cavalry were sent after them, followed by three legions. Except for the rearguard, which put up a stubborn fight, the rest of the Gauls in front tried to escape once they heard the din of battle being joined behind them. Without any concerted plan, the tribesmen were completely vulnerable and the Romans were at liberty to kill as many as they could reach. Only nightfall stopped the slaughter and the Romans returned to their camp.

Caesar marched on into the territory of the Belgae, securing submissions as he went; first the Suessiones, then the Bellovaci and the Ambiani. It was the last of those who were neighbours to the Nervii, a fierce warrior people, who claimed they would rather accept death than Roman domination and rebuked their fellow-countrymen for having done so.

Determined to crush all resistance, the Romans marched northward to the river Sambre, where intelligence indicated that the Nervii and two other tribes, the Atrebates and the Viromandui, were concentrating. The Nervii were expecting the Roman column to arrive with each legion separated by a baggage train, so that they would be able to take on a single legion whilst the others were still some distance away. Their information was totally incorrect, for the column was headed by six legions without baggage, followed by all the force's transport train with a rearguard of two more legions.

First contact with the enemy was made by the cavalry, archers and slingers, who were ahead of the main column. These crossed the river and engaged in skirmishes with the enemy horse. They failed to observe the main force of tribesmen, who were lying concealed in thick woods at the top of the hillside where their horsemen were keeping the Roman cavalry busy.

The first legions arrived at the river late in the day and set about the construction of their night camp. The Nervii, watching from their concealed position and no doubt surprised by the size of the legionary force, nevertheless decided to attack whilst the Romans were occupied with construction work and not expecting a major assault. Once they could see the head of the baggage train in the distance and knew thereby that the remaining legions were too far away to be of immediate assistance to their fellows, they charged out from the woods, putting the cavalry to flight. They then made for the river and were across before the Romans realised what was happening, stunned by the speed of the tribesmen.

Caesar was taken completely by surprise and he had no time to arrange his troops in an orderly battle line. Recovery from the shock of the attack was largely due to the experience of the soldiers, which enabled them to keep cool heads, and to the fact that the legionary commanders were under orders to remain with their units until the camp site was ready for occupation.

On Caesar's side of the field, the troops had managed to get themselves into a reasonable line and were ready for the Nervii when the attack came. Caesar then went to the other end of the field, but found that the men were already in action. The assault had been so rapid that they were still encumbered with their shield covers and were fighting unhelmeted.

LEGIONES IX and X, who were holding the left, succeeded in driving the

PLATE 5   An *imaginifer* watches Roman troops about to engage some hostiles as a cavalry signifer approaches. Britain, late first century AD

The *imaginifer*, or bearer of the Emperor's Image (*imago*), is wearing the same cape shoulder-doubling as the cavalry and other standard-bearers are known to have done; because the man is an infantry standard-bearer, the body of the mail is longer than that of cavalry hauberks. The figure is based on a cast of the *stela* of the *Imaginifer* Genialis, who served with COHORS VII RAETORUM; perhaps because the unit was an auxiliary one, his helmet had no mask, unlike legionary examples. This aspect was probably associated with 'citizen' status, for the cavalry *signifer* belonged to a unit whose titles make it clear that, though it was a cavalry regiment, it had been granted Roman citizenship *en bloc*. This status may also be reflected by the elaborate cresting of the helmet of the *signifer*, which figure is based on the *stela* of the *Signifer* Flavinus, who served with the thousand-strong ALA AUGUSTA GALLORUM PETRIANA MILLIARIA CIVIUM ROMANORUM; the stone may now be seen in Hexham Abbey. The rider's body defence is the same as that of the auxiliary infantry of the first century AD: short sleeves and no doubling for the shoulders. It may be presumed that there were small slits at either side of the lower edge of the mail, as with all other cavalry hauberks, in order that the mail would be sufficiently free for riding. He also wears *feminalia*, which had seemingly become the normal wear for all auxiliaries; again, this piece of apparel may have been worn according to the climate, but one imagines that cavalrymen would have been more likely to require them than the infantry.

Atrebates back down to the river and killed a great many as they stumbled through the water. The legionaries then pursued the rest across the river and put them to flight on the far bank. Likewise LEGIONES XI and VIII managed to repel the Viromandui and chased them down to the river. In both cases, the tribesmen were out of breath, having run at great speed over a long distance, and were attacking up hill in some places, which was a disadvantage under normal circumstances.

But on the Roman right, LEGIONES XII and VII bore the brunt of the attack by the Nervii, who began to surround the two legions with large numbers. The situation had become so desperate by the time Caesar reached them that LEGIO XII was so confined by the enemy that the men had no room to fight properly and all the centurions of COHORS IV were dead, as well as the standard bearer. The other cohorts were in little better case, with almost all of their centurions among the casualties. Some of the men were even falling back and beginning to retreat, when Caesar snatched a shield from a man at the rear and managed to make his way to the front lines, calling to the surviving centurions and ordering the troops to open their ranks and give themselves room to use their swords. The commander's presence lifted the spirits of the badly shaken soldiers and the ferocious attack of the Nervii was checked and began to slow down.

Observing that LEGIO VII was also in trouble, Caesar ordered the two legions to form a square, so preventing the Nervii from surrounding the rear and enabling them to fight in any direction.

At that point, the two rearguard legions arrived on the scene and LEGIO X, the pursuit of the Atrebates apparently over, was returned to the main battle. So heartened by the relieving force were the battle-weary legionaries, that even those who were wounded found renewed strength and rejoined the fray, even if some of them had to support themselves with their shields to do so.

With victory clearly in sight, all the Roman side made even greater efforts to conclude the business. The Nervii fought back against the overwhelming odds with enormous courage, even clambering onto the mounds of their own dead to hurl back the spears thrown at them. When finally all was still and the Romans moved among the heaps of dead flesh, collecting the weapons of the fallen and removing the thousands of bodies, it must have become apparent to them then that almost all the Nervii had perished in the battle. Later, it was reported that of their 60,000 warriors, there were but 500 men left alive or uninjured.

By 55 BC, all Gaul was quiet, but another Germanic invasion had commenced; on that occasion the threat was in the north and towards the territory of the Belgae. Caesar, realising that the Gauls, by their very nature, would be unlikely to prevent the Germans from carrying out their intentions of settling in that region, at once marched to intercept them. As he approached, German envoys began to arrive with the request that they should be permitted to settle in Gaul, since they had been forced to migrate by other tribes east of the Rhine.

Caesar became convinced that the German envoys were simply delaying any action on his part until such time as their cavalry, which had mostly crossed the river Meuse in search of plunder and forage, returned and rejoined their forces. Though not impressed by their duplicity, Caesar arranged to meet as many of their headmen as would come before him, when his army had encamped at the nearest source of water, which happened to be somewhat closer to their encampment. He ordered his cavalry, which preceded the infantry column, not to engage the enemy, even if provoked. But once the Roman cavalry came within sight of some

Vexillum, based on the remains of a flag standard from Egypt, now in the collection of the Museum of Fine Arts, Moscow. Probably third century AD. Author's reconstruction.

German horse, who had remained on their side of the Meuse, they immediately attacked the Romans, despite being outnumbered by six to one. The sudden and unexpected action by the Germans threw them into disarray and though they managed to recover themselves, the German riders jumped down from their mounts and began bringing the Romans down by the simple expedient of wounding their horses in the belly. Those that were not killed, panicked and fled back to the infantry column, harried as they went.

The attack on the cavalry made it plain to Caesar that there could be no further delay in bringing the Germans to battle and he continued his march towards them, making camp that night as he had planned. The following day, the German leaders presented themselves at the Roman camp as arranged, hoping to persuade Caesar to overlook the attack on his cavalry and gain more time for theirs to return from foraging. They were all promptly arrested and Caesar ordered the advance against their encampment.

The Germans, now leaderless, had little cohesion. Those who managed to arm themselves fought back desperately, whilst their families tried to escape into the countryside. The Roman cavalry, however, were waiting for them and a terrible massacre began, at the sight and sound of which the German warriors who were still fighting lost all heart for the fray and retreated in haste towards the Rhine with the Roman cavalry in pursuit. Trapped against the Rhine and Moselle rivers, many were cut down; others who tried to swim to safety were drowned, exhausted by the rout.

In order to discourage further Germanic incursions into Gaul and upon an appeal from the German tribe of the Ubii, who were Roman allies, to 'show the flag' on the east side of the Rhine as a warning to the Suebi to desist from attacking them, Caesar then entered upon a remarkable bridge-building project, which in itself would impress the Germans by its display of Roman capability.

Disliking the idea of using a pontoon bridge and thinking it too dangerous for that method to be employed over such a wide and fast-flowing river; Caesar ordered his engineers to devise a safer solution to the problem. They achieved a design which consisted of a series of double piles arranged in pairs, with beams laid between them transversely to the direction of the bridge. Longitudinal timbers were then laid over the beams, with a further layer of poles in the transverse attitude to them and bundles of sticks forming the surface of the roadway.

The double piles were braced against the strong current with diagonal timbers on the downstream side, and to prevent the bridge being damaged by objects floating down the river, in front of each of the pile piers three vertical timbers were erected in a triangular plan, a short distance away on the upstream side.

To construct that ingenious bridge, which was probably about 0.5 km (⅓ mi) in length, a massive amount of timber had to be collected and at least one great floating pile-driver built, before the actual work started on the structure. Such was the highly organised and competent way in which Caesar's soldiers worked that the entire undertaking was completed in only ten days.

Caesar took his army across the Rhine and spent several days devastating the territory of the Sugambri, who had gone into hiding upon hearing of Caesar's bridging of the Rhine. He then proceeded to the lands of the Ubii and upon being informed that a large force was concentrating in the middle of the territory of the Suebi, with the intention of engaging the Romans, if they should dare to enter their lands, he moved his army back into Gaul, destroying the bridge as he went.

Whilst Caesar wrote that he had done all that honour and Roman interests required, his withdrawal does seem to have been much the better part of valour.

Gaius Julius Caesar Octavianus Augustus
63 BC—AD 14

Gaius Octavius, or Augustus as he was later to become known to the world, was born in the small town of *Velitrae* on 23 September 63 BC, the son of Gaius Octavius and his wife Atia, the niece of the Dictator Gaius Julius Caesar.

The long and troubled years which followed saw the rise of Caesar and his great triumphs, the tragedy of the civil war with Pompeius and the eventual assassination of the Dictator at the pinnacle of his power. Adopted in Caesar's will, Gaius Julius Caesar Octavianus, as he now became, had grown into a young man of slender, almost feminine appearance, but possessed of a quality of mind which set him apart from ordinary mortals.

With the lessons of Caesar's life and downfall clearly impressed on his mind, Octavianus set out on a road by which he could gain total control over the direction of the Roman world and establish Italy as the supreme nation in the Mediterranean area. But it was a road upon which there

---

PLATE 6   An *aquilifer*, from the victorious force under the command of Antonius Primus, tears the *imago* of Aulus Vitellius from a standard after the destruction of Cremona, AD 69

The *aquilifer* wears a corselet of silvered bronze *squamae* over an arming doublet with a single-layer kilt and upper arm defences of *pteruges* which may have been made of either leather or linen. The size of the scales of the corselet are shown in this illustration as they appear on the grave *stela* of Lucius Sertorius Firmus, an *aquilifer* who served with LEGIO XI PIA FIDELIS, in the collection of the Verona Museum; it is probable that these rather large scales would have been smaller in fact, the sculptural representation having been so cut for ease of execution. Whilst the *stela* also shows the *aquilifer* carrying his sword on his left side, it is quite probable that such men, including centurions, in fact carried their swords on the right; the

reason for this phenomenon is thought by some to be the aesthetic balance desired by the sculptor. The same observation may be made with regard to the *stela* of *Centurio* Marcus Favonius Facilis, in the collection of the Colchester and Essex Museum, Colchester, England. In sculpture, the *aquilifer* is shown bare-headed, a fact which does not apply to other standard-bearers. The significance of this, and there presumably is a meaning, is not known at this time; however, it is scarcely credible that *aquiliferi* went into action without any form of head defence, especially since they were usually at the forefront of the battle.
The *signifer* who is watching the *aquilifer* is based on the grave *stela* of Quintus Luccius Faustus in the

collection of the Mittelrheinisches Landesmuseum, Mainz. The standard-bearer wears a *lorica hamata*, similar to those of the cavalry of the period, but with a double kilt and upper arm defences of *pteruges*. The *stela* of Faustus clearly depicts a masked helmet with a pointed diadem similar to the Cavalry Sports type 'B' skull-piece from Newstead, Scotland, in the collection of the National Museum of the Antiquities of Scotland, Edinburgh. The *signum* (standard) carries six *phalerae*, which may possibly indicate that he belonged to the sixth *centuria* of his *cohors*; a second, almost identical *stela* shows the same type of standard with only a pair of *phalerae*.

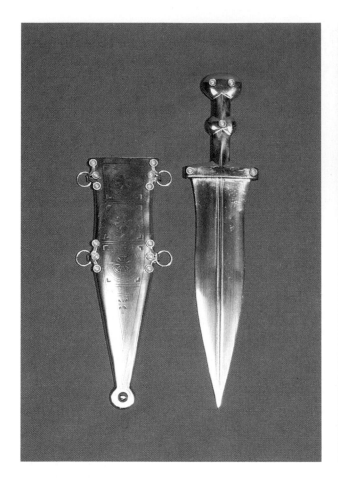
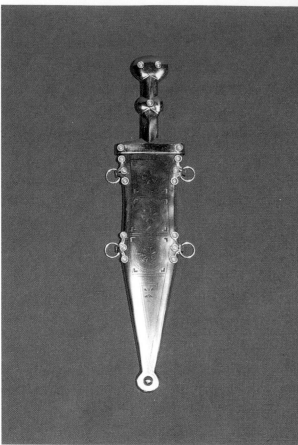

could be no opposition, open or secret, and in dealing with opponents real or imagined, Octavianus sometimes exhibited a degree of ruthlessness which betrayed a deep-seated fear of conspiracy and assassination.

The rift between Octavianus and Marcus Antonius, which finally came to a head in 32 BC, was a clear illustration of his aims. Dedicated to Italian dominion, he could never have accepted the ambitions of Queen Cleopatra, so desirous of expanding Egyptian influence in the Middle East. For that reason and the influence the Queen held over Antonius, the war which terminated in the deaths of both Antonius and Cleopatra at Alexandria may be seen as having been directed more against Egyptian expansionism; though the matter may have been somewhat inflamed by moral differences between Octavianus and Antonius. The rigid small-town morality of the 'old' Roman, which meant a high regard for the family unit, was very much a part of the character of Octavianus; not so Antonius, the big, bluff hard-drinker with the more earthy nature.

With the Egyptian affair over, the year 30 BC saw Octavianus astride the Roman world like a colossus and the following year he celebrated a triple triumph in Rome. At long last the Romans had peace and the gates of the temple of Janus, kept open in time of war, were closed for the third time in

Infantry dagger and scabbard with inlaid decoration, based on a specimen found at Utrecht, now in the Rijksmuseum G.M. Kam, Nijmegen, Netherlands. All scabbards of this type seem to have been decorated. Late first century BC to first century AD.

60

Locket of a cavalry *spatha* with decoration of Thracian origin. See overleaf for detailed drawing of the original.

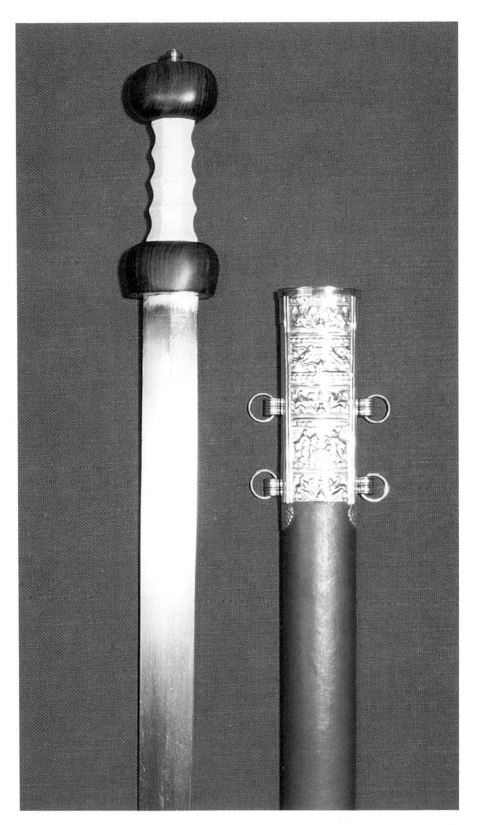

Rome's violent history. The title *imperator*, signifying his personal authority over the army, was granted to him by the Senate, to be placed in front of his ordinary names. The following year, he held a *census* of Roman citizens and took the title of *princeps*, meaning in this case 'foremost man'.

Though the goodwill of the vast majority of people had obviously been gained by the state of peace which he had brought about, aided by generosity to the army and a policy of cheap food supplies; Octavianus realised that too blatant a display of personal power could incur the same dire consequences as had been visited upon his grand-uncle Caesar. So on the first day of 27 BC, he laid down all the powers which he had exercised as a member of the Second Triumvirate and insisted that whatever powers the

Sword and scabbard of Augustan date, based on a blade from Chichester, Sussex, England, and the remains of a scabbard found at Mainz, now in the Römisch-Germanisches Zentralmuseum, Mainz, Germany. Author's reconstruction.

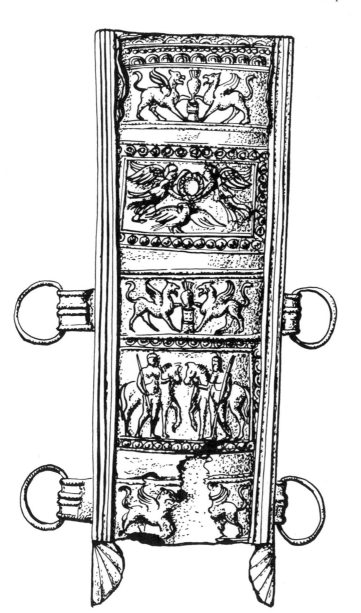

Locket from the scabbard of a cavalry *spatha*, with decoration of Thracian type, from Pettau (Ptuj), Yugoslavia, the ancient *Poetovio*. Scabbards with separate lockets and chapes, similar to those of the *gladius*, probably appeared during the first half of the first century AD.

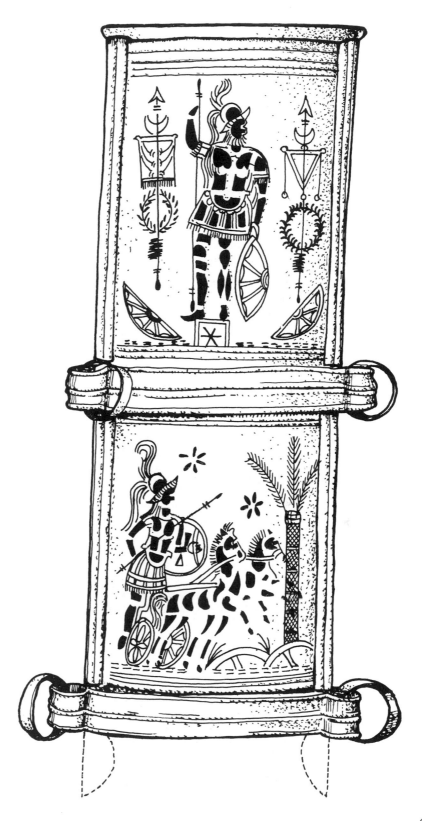

Locket of a Pompeii-pattern *gladius* scabbard, pierced and engraved with figures of the war god Mars. Though never represented in sculpture, scabbards with mounts of this type were extremely common from the early first century AD onward.

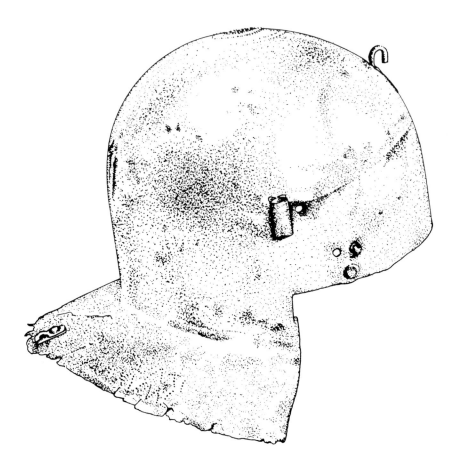

Crude bronze infantry helmet skull made by metal spinning. The helmet carried a crest and side-plumes, but belonged to an auxiliary soldier. Possibly made during the first half of the first century AD. Private collection.

Senate chose to confer upon him should be limited to a set term of years as Consul with the powers of a Tribune of the people.

In that way Octavianus appeared to gratify Republican sentiments, whilst retaining the powers which made him a monarch in all but name. According to the historian Tacitus, so many of those who might have opposed him had died during the civil war and those of the upper class who were left found that they profited by his rule; so Octavianus was able to proceed with his design without opposition. It was considered by the Senate that a new title should be awarded to him and eventually the name of *Augustus* was chosen. It was a name devoid of military associations or kingly inference, being derived from antique religious meaning in the field of augury, which had come to mean 'dignified' by religious association.

To maintain his personal control of the army, he divided the governor-ship of the provinces between the Senate and himself, which gave the appearance of acquiescence to the will of the people, but at the same time ensured that the provinces under his control, through *legati* appointed by him, were those where attack by other nations was most likely and were thus those where the largest number of troops were concentrated.

At the termination of the civil war, Augustus had inherited an enormous force of 60 legions. These he reduced to a mere 28, which was to remain

64

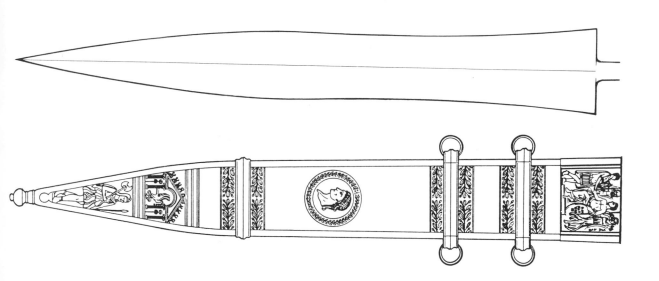

Restored blade and scabbard of the sword of Tiberius in the collection of the British Museum. Probably manufactured late in 15 BC, the piece may have been one of several issued to officers who took part in the subjugation of the Vindelici.

Scutum of the second half of the first century BC, based on the dimensions of an example from Kasr el Harit in the Fayum, Egypt, and an iron boss-plate from Mainz. Author's reconstruction.

the normal complement, with new legions being raised or others destroyed or disbanded, as circumstances dictated. He also introduced regular annual recruitment of auxiliary forces. These had previously been allies or mercenaries employed for individual campaigns, fighting with their own native equipment (the *sagittarii* continued to do so even when they had been absorbed into the Roman army). The infantry and cavalry were supplied with equipment of Roman pattern and the units were organised after the Roman manner; though for reasons of manufacture, the disappearance of native arms was probably quite gradual.

The traditional reward of land grants to time-expired legionary soldiers, though by no means terminated during Augustus' reign, became difficult to fulfil. The alternative was to award a monetary substitute and to that end, Augustus founded the *aerarium militare,* or military treasury, supplied with funds from taxation sources.

Since his health was a constant problem to him, Augustus was never a great field commander. He took part in only two campaigns, apart from the defeat of Marcus Antonius at *Mutina* in 43 BC, where he was said to have displayed considerable courage when the *aquilifer* of his legion was incapacitated by wounds, taking up and carrying the Eagle himself. In his youth, he was quite severely injured in a campaign against the Dalmatians, having both arms and one leg crushed by the collapse of a bridge. The injury to his leg may have persisted, since he was reported to have had a slight limp.

All further campaigns were conducted by others under his direction, especially by members of the Imperial family. The main theatre for his policy of expansion was the region to the north of the Adriatic Sea, up to the Danube river and into present-day southern Germany, the Roman provinces of *Pannonia, Noricum* and *Raetia.* The conquest of those territories between 16 and 9 BC was undertaken by his stepsons, Tiberius and Drusus. Further expansion into western Czechoslovakia was in progress in AD 6,

65

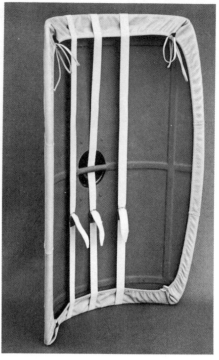

Author's reconstruction of a shield cover (*tegimen*), based on fragments from the site of the fortress of *Vindonissa* (Windisch), Switzerland. The shield form probably dates from the late first century BC and was superseded during the first half of the following century.

when the provinces of *Pannonia* and *Illyricum* broke into a serious revolt, which it took Tiberius three years to put down. No sooner was the revolt over than news of an unimaginable disaster reached Augustus. Three legions, LEGIONES XVII, XVIII and XIX, the general staff and their auxiliaries had been ambushed in the Teutoburg Forest by the German chieftain Arminius and almost totally annihilated.

The shock to Augustus was very deep and there was even a fear that the populace in Rome might attempt to overthrow him. He did not shave or cut his hair for months afterwards and often cried out to the dead commander of that luckless army, Quinctilius Varus (husband of a grand-niece of Augustus), to restore his legions to him. The loss of those units, one tenth of Rome's legionary strength, was so serious that all thoughts of further expansion were abandoned at that time. Germanicus, the son of Drusus, headed a punitive expedition across the Rhine and had the grim task of collecting the remains of the fallen men of the three legions.

In AD 14, Augustus was returning to Rome from Capri, when he was taken ill with a stomach complaint which had troubled him a number of times during his life; but on that occasion it was to be the last and he expired at *Nola* on 14 August in the same room, allegedly, as his father had done. His body was conveyed to Rome and cremated on the Field of Mars. The ashes were placed in the great mausoleum which he had built many years earlier; the remains of the building may still be seen today in the City of Rome, near to another of his monuments, the *Ara Pacis*, the Altar of Peace.

The Claudian Invasion of Britain

AD 43

The political situation in Britain by the year AD 42 had become progressively more anti-Roman, particularly, it appears, with the death or disabling ill-health of Cunobelinus, King of the powerful tribe of the Catuvellauni, whose influence spread over a wide area of East Anglia, down to the Thames valley; their tribal capital at the time of the Roman invasion being at *Camulodunon*, in the region of modern Colchester.

Cunobelinus had maintained at least peaceful relations with other tribal Kings, both 'client' Roman and those opposed to any Romano-British developments, perhaps fearing that Rome would if necessary, intervene with force to protect her client monarchs and interests of trade. His two sons, Togodumnus and Caratacus, clearly felt no such trepidation and once their father's restraining hand was removed, they began to move against the client Kings, causing two of them to quit Britain and seek Roman support.

The first of these was their brother Adminius, who had tried to persuade the insane Emperor Gaius to invade the island, with ludicrous results. The second was Verica of the Atrebates. Whilst actual evidence is extremely sparse regarding the cause of Verica's supplication to the Emperor Claudius in AD 41, logic makes it reasonable to suppose that it was the action of Caratacus, who thus extended his tribe's influence southward to the Regni.

Trade with the pro-Roman tribes in Britain would certainly have revealed the mineral resources of the country and that, coupled with the necessity of direct action against the hostile tribal leaders, was probably the main reason for the Roman decision to invade. It has, however, been suggested that Claudius' own position, which appears to have been rather weak at that time, would have benefited from such a conquest.

Claudius, the most unlikely of Imperial figures, had never had any military experience; in fact he was physically such an unprepossessing individual that his own family preferred to keep him out of the public eye. However, upon the assassination of his nephew Gaius Caesar, there was no alternative candidate for the position of Emperor left alive and the Praetorian Guard duly acclaimed him, despite attempts by the Consuls and the City militia to restore the Republic. So possibly a military victory, even if it was won against a relatively 'soft' target, would have improved his prestige.

The actual invasion of Britain is a subject which must, at this time, be reconstructed by the use of logic, working with the very few clues provided

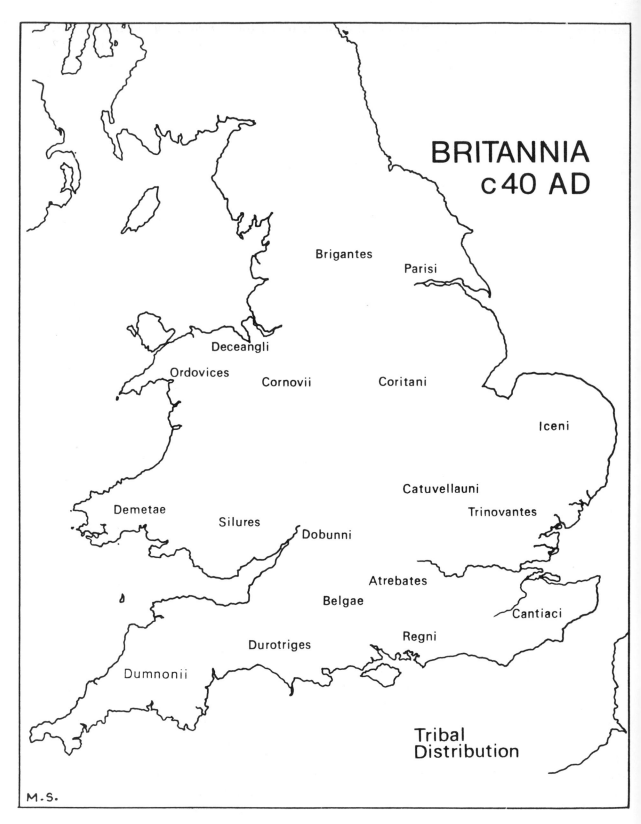

BRITANNIA
c 40 AD

Brigantes

Parisi

Deceangli

Ordovices

Cornovii

Coritani

Iceni

Demetae

Silures

Dobunni

Catuvellauni

Trinovantes

Atrebates

Belgae

Cantiaci

Regni

Durotriges

Dumnonii

Tribal
Distribution

M·S·

by archaeological excavation and the *Roman History* of Dio Cassius. The latter work, though apparently containing many errors, was probably based upon the *Annals* of Tacitus, which sadly has not come down to us in its entirety; the period between the death of the Emperor Tiberius and the sixth year of the reign of Claudius, which would have covered the invasion, remains lost.

Three of the legions which took part in the operation were stationed on the Rhine frontier: LEGIO II AUGUSTA at *Argentorate* (Strasbourg), LEGIO XIIII GEMINA at *Moguntiacum* (Mainz) and LEGIO XX VALERIA at *Novaesium* (Neuss). The fourth regiment, LEGIO IX HISPANA, was probably stationed at *Siscia* (Sisak, near Zagreb) and was obliged to undertake the long journey westward to the Gallic coast, almost 800 miles in a direct line to the embarkation port of *Gesoriacum* (Boulogne). The legion may have been transported by ship at least part of the way to their destination, which would have spared both the soldiers and many thousands of bootnails.

It has been suggested that *vexillationes* (detachments) from at least one other legion took part in the initial stage of the operation, and slight though the evidence is for such an addition, the possibility should not be discounted.

We are not told by what route the Rhine legions were moved to *Gesoriacum*, but they were most probably transported down the Rhine by ship to the North Sea and then southward along the coast to the Dover Strait; the only objection to this being the dangers inherent in marine transport of so large a number of men and animals.

The final shape of the *scutum*, introduced in the first century AD. The bronze edging was later carried out in rawhide, probably because of economic necessity. Author's reconstructon.

Once the entire force was assembled at the embarkation point, the spectacle must have been awesome. The total numbers, including the auxiliary units, were in the region of 40,000 combat troops, to which must be added the *calones* (camp servants) and other non-combatants, such as field dressers, medical staff, clerks, etc.

The departure of the forces from *Gesoriacum* became subject to delay, because of the ill-health of Lucius Sulpicius Galba, the same Galba later to become Emperor, whom Claudius wished to take with him to Britain, once the army commander, Aulus Plautius Silvanus, had achieved a firm hold on the island's south-eastern territory. Other, perhaps more plausible explanations for the delay may be found today; however, that given was the official Roman story.

The length of time which elapsed must be measured in months, rather than weeks, because we are told that it was rather late in the campaigning season that the orders to proceed were received by Plautius. Certainly it was sufficient time for fear, born of superstition and uncertainty in face of the open sea, to spread amongst the troops, with the result that the force refused to carry out the mission. Plautius was quite unable to persuade them otherwise; no doubt he was unused to indiscipline, especially on so large a scale, and was obliged to appeal to Rome for guidance.

Claudius duly dispatched his Greek adviser, an ex-slave named Narcissus, to deal with the problem. He was evidently a poor choice of envoy to be entrusted with the task of regaining the confidence of tough, proud frontier troops and it nearly proved fatal for him. The soldiers, no doubt the citizen legionaries in the main, were furious at being addressed by a freed-man and drowned his attempts at a speech in derision. One may imagine the cat-calls and obscenities which greeted him; if it had not been for the sense of humour of one of the men, Narcissus would have been fortunate to escape with his life. It was the Roman custom to allow slaves to dress up in their masters' clothes at the festival of Saturnalia and ape their functions. Seeing Narcissus, the ex-slave, standing before him on the camp rostrum, the nameless comedian could not resist the parallel and shouted out, 'It's Saturnalia!' The host's anger simply dissolved into thousands of belly-laughs and Narcissus was safe, even allowed to deliver his address without further interruption. We have no transcript of his speech, but it was well enough received to restore the army to a war footing and the lading of the transports was completed in readiness for sailing.

Dio Cassius wrote that the invasion fleet sailed in three divisions, which statement can be interpreted in at least two ways. It has been considered to mean that the divisions landed at three different points on the Kent coast, thought to have been *Rutupiae* (Richborough), *Lemanis* (Lympne) and *Dubris* (Dover). However, it would clearly have been necessary for the

---

PLATE 7   Activity in a fort of semi-permanent construction. Second half of the first century AD

The *centurio* is based on the grave *stela* of Marcus Favonius Facilis in the collection of the Colchester and Essex Museum, Colchester, England. Facilis died before AD 60, when his grave *stela* was overturned in the Boudican destruction of *Camulodunum*. He wears a *lorica hamata* with deltoid and abdominal extensions, which probably involved some 'tailoring' of the mail. The *pteruges* are in this case only a single layer to the upper arm, whilst the kilt is doubled. The greaves (*ocreae*) are of a plain anatomical type; others were clearly embossed with quite elaborate designs. The symbol of this officer's rank is the *vitis* (vine staff); unlike modern armies wherein it is an offence to strike a subordinate, the *centurio* was permitted to mete out on-the-spot justice to recalcitrant soldiers under his command. Facilis, it appears, never managed to achieve great deeds during his career, for there are no representations of military *dona* (decorations) on his *stela*; these would most certainly have been shown had he possessed any. His

helmet is of Imperial Gallic type 'D', after a fine specimen from the river Rhine at Weisenau, unfortunately destroyed in World War II. The great *crista transversa* of feathers is another mark of the man's rank; these were also made from horse-hair.

The legionary infantryman being upbraided by the *centurio* is largely based on the *stela* of Gaius Valerius Crispus from Wiesbaden, Germany, in the collection of the Städtisches Museum, Wiesbaden. This figure clearly shows that mail hauberks were still being worn by legionaries during the second half of the first century AD. Whilst the *stela* shows what appear to be *feminalia* coated with *pteruges*, this phenomenon is probably the result of the manner in which the *stela* was marked out prior to the sculptor commencing his work. A simple human form was laid out and cut up to the bifurcation; any *pteruges* which came below that point were simply worked round the thighs. This may be more clearly seen on the representation of Deus Martius, inlaid into a sword-blade fragment from the site of the fort at

Arbeia (South Shields) on Hadrian's Wall.

The figure descending the stairway (*ascensus*) is an auxiliary infantryman of a COHORS RAETORUM, based on the *stela* of Firmus in the Rheinisches Landesmuseum, Bonn. Many of the auxiliaries owned belts and sidearms which were very splendid indeed; in fact, they seem to have outshone their legionary counterparts in this respect. The figure wears a *paenula*, a cloak of semi-circular form, which also had a pointed hood. Cloaks of this pattern were extremely common in the Roman army and appear to have been preferred to the *sagum*, which was of simple rectangular form; the latter were usually worn by the officers. Auxiliaries are shown to carry *hastae* (thrusting spears), sometimes in pairs and in one case a single spear and two small javelins; the heavy javelins were the pole weapon of the legionary. The shield is the oval *clipeus*, carried by both infantry and cavalry in the *auxilia*.

Romans to have established a beach-head at a sufficiently safe haven for the reception of troop reinforcements and the heavy equipment, in order that the latter did not have to lie off the coast in what were known to be treacherous waters as far as the weather was concerned. It is therefore more likely that the three divisions in fact landed at one point, most probably Rutupiae with its superior harbour, with a time lapse between each of the elements to allow for the beach-head to be secured against what was probably expected to be quite ferocious opposition.

To their surprise, and doubtless relief, the Romans found the landing area unoccupied and they were able to effect what could have been a very bloody assault without hindrance. The absence of opposition is thought to have been caused by the lengthy delay in the mounting of the operation by the Romans and, indeed, this does seem to be very likely. However, the main reason for the withdrawal may perhaps have been the urgent demands of the agricultural calendar, rather than a belief that the invasion had been postponed until the following year. It is difficult to believe that the British made no effort to gather intelligence concerning the Roman activities in Gaul, or that they were unable to do so; they would therefore have been apprised of the final preparations of the invasion fleet.

If so, the British were faced with a dilemma. Either they were to take the Romans at a disadvantage in attempting to land and push them back into the sea, which would mean losing much of their harvest and consequent starvation; or they were to return home and gather their crops, hoping to make use of the natural defences of the country, such as rivers and swamps, so as to avoid a pitched battle which they probably knew they would lose, whilst making harassing moves in an attempt to discourage the invaders from pursuing their aim. The latter appears from subsequent events to have been the case.

Unfortunately we probably will never know what was in the British leaders' minds until the lost part of the *Annals* comes to light. But it is certain that Plautius took full advantage of his good fortune and began his advance into the interior, hoping to come to grips with the British as he did so. The British leaders had, in the meantime, managed to assemble some numbers to the east of the river Medway, but they evidently felt them to be too few for any kind of serious attack upon the advancing Roman columns and simply melted away into the forests and swamps if the Romans went in pursuit of them.

Plautius continued his march westwards until he reached the first natural obstacle, a river, thought to have been the Medway. The main force of the Britons had now arrived and encamped in a careless fashion on the opposing bank, confident in the belief that the Romans would be unable to cross the river and attack them without the aid of a bridge; clearly the British leadership had little idea of Roman military practices.

Plautius decided to employ a tried and tested method of deception, rather than attempt to bridge the river and engage the enemy by simple frontal assault. Further upstream from the main area of confrontation, the

Sword and scabbard, late first century BC to early first century AD, based on the specimen recovered from the river Thames at Fulham, London, now in the British Museum, and a face-plate of similar pattern, in the Rijksmuseum van Oudheden, Leiden, Netherlands.

Bronze cavalry helmet of Sports type 'D', pre-dating AD 45, found at Vize, Thrace. The helmet was either completely or partially silvered. In the collection of the Archaeological Museum, Istanbul.

72

73

Romans discovered that there was a fordable point which enabled Plautius to place a force of legionary infantry on the opposing side of the river. LEGIO II AUGUSTA, under the command of the future Emperor, Titus Flavius Vespasianus, was certainly used for that purpose and possibly a detachment of one of the other three legions on the first day of the battle.

Whilst the legionary force made its way across, no doubt with as much stealth as possible, perhaps by muffling their equipment, a unit of Batavian cavalry, famous for their ability to swim rivers in full battle order (though one suspects that a heavy mail hauberk would have been most dangerous in that regard), held the attention of the tribesmen by swimming the quite wide reach of the river, apparently surprising the Britons totally. Instead of attacking the warriors, the Batavians directed their attention to the chariot ponies, thereby depriving the enemy of their mobile arm and forcing them to alter their normal battle method.

The loss of mobility was made all the worse by the sudden and unexpected appearance of LEGIO II AUGUSTA on their right flank. Remarkably, the tribesmen recovered rapidly from those two unpleasant surprises and joined battle with the legionaries with what seems, in view of their vastly inferior arms and training, singular courage. The Romans, who probably began their assault early in the morning, were unable to rout the British and the action was broken off as darkness fell. The following day, another legion, probably LEGIO XX VALERIA, under the command of C. Hosidius Geta,

PLATE 8   Legionary infantry engage Dacian warriors during the first Trajanic campaign. Early second century AD

The legionary infantryman wearing a plain *lorica hamata* is based on the grave *stela* of Gaius Castricius in the collection of the Aquincum Museum, Budapest, where the stele was found. This provides evidence of the continued use of mail by the western legions in the second century AD, since the legion with which Castricius served, LEGIO II ADIUTRIX, is thought to have first been stationed at *Aquincum* in 106. His bronze helmet is of Imperial Gallic type 'I', which class of helmet was probably made at the end of the civil war of AD 68–69. The most interesting feature of the *stela* is the belt groin-guard unit; the fittings clearly represented by the sculptor bear a remarkably close resemblance to those which were excavated from *Herculaneum* in company with the corpse of their unfortunate owner, who was probably killed during the second eruption of Mount Vesuvius, which also destroyed the town of

Pompeii. The accuracy of the belt-fittings is such that the sword baldric, which displays a continuous line of metal discs, is probably equally truthful. Absolutely no attempt was made to depict a baldric fastener and it may be that many of the objects which have long been thought to serve that function are probably parts of cavalry harnesses. Castricius also carries a *clipeus* shield with a 'Medusa' boss, which is something of a departure from our conception of legionary equipment, though known from one other stele of legionary origin, that of Publius Flavoleius Cordus, who served with LEGIO XIIII GEMINA; however, since Cordus has what is thought to be a bronze discharge diploma tucked in his tunic belt, he may have been of non-citizen origin, but served his time as an auxiliary and then joined a legion, the shield shape serving to attest the fact.

The second legionary wears a

lorica segmentata of Newstead pattern, named after the quantity of cuirass fragments found at Newstead, Scotland (National Museum of the Antiquities of Scotland). All the intricate hinges and buckles of the earlier patterns have gone; the collar has become a solid unit and the lower pair of girdle plates have been made into a single deep element. The simplification of the cuirass meant a valuable saving in manufacture and this is the type of cuirass to be seen in the majority of the representations of legionary infantry on Trajan's Column. The helmet is of Imperial Gallic type 'J', drawn from the specimen found on the site of the fort of *Brigetio* in Hungary. Though described as of Gallic type, the piece may be of Italian origin.

The legionaries carry *pila* with heavy lead loads; thrown at close range, these javelins could pierce an adversary's shield and body armour.

crossed the river and with the combined legionary forces, the Romans succeeded in defeating the British, who fell back as best they could to the river Thames, with the Roman cavalry hot on their heels.

Since they were familiar with the marshes and mud-flats, probably in the region of present-day Westminster, the tribesmen were able to cross to the farther side without difficulty; the Romans attempted to follow them, but found themselves trapped in the dangerous ground and lost some men. One may conjecture that the remains of the lost riders and their mounts may still be buried and perhaps well-preserved in the ground under the south bank.

Precisely what happened next at the river Thames is in some doubt, but it is certain that Plautius' advance was halted there in accordance with Imperial orders, to await the arrival of the Emperor, who was to lead the army in person against the Catuvellaunian capital of *Camulodunon*. The flagging British resolve to resist after their defeat at the Medway allegedly received a boost from the death of King Togodumnus during the period that elapsed before the arrival of Claudius from Rome; however, the King may have been killed in action at the Medway, or succumbed to wounds shortly thereafter. Whatever the case, the British cause was now solely in the hands of his brother Caratacus, a brave and able man, who realised that the tribesmen would not be able to confront the Roman army again and withdrew himself and his family to Wales in order to continue the resistance.

The Emperor with his entourage finally arrived at the camp of Plautius, after a most hazardous voyage from Rome, and took command of the assembled forces. He then led the army across the river Thames, which Dio Cassius describes as a stream, and was clearly both narrower and shallower than it is today, now that the soldiers had had time to prepare a suitable surface over the mud-flats.

Whether or not the British put up any serious resistance to the advance on *Camulodunon* is questionable; after their sound defeat at the Medway and in face of such a large force, without any natural barriers of consequence to hinder them, surely only the most determined and the foolhardy would have sought to continue the conflict any further at that time. The ancient writers do not mention any attempt to hold the capital against Claudius, and he there received the submission of eleven British Kings. The whole period of the Emperor's presence in Britain probably amounted to no more than four weeks, perhaps less; but the conquest was not to be concluded until AD 84.

The subjugation of the remainder of the south and south-west of Britain probably began before the Emperor's brief visit to the new province and was conducted by Vespasianus and his command, LEGIO II AUGUSTA. According to the Roman historian Gaius Suetonius Tranquillus (known to us simply as Suetonius) in his surviving work *The Twelve Caesars* Vespasianus fought thirty battles during the campaign, captured more than twenty towns, conquered the Isle of Wight and subjugated two warlike tribes.

An officer and members of the Praetorian Guard. Note the early pattern of *scutum* being carried by the men; the relief dates from the late first century AD. In the collection of the Vatican Museums, Rome.

The most impressive of the places which he assaulted at that time may still be seen today, the great Durotrigian hill-fort of *Mai-dun*, or Maiden Castle as we know it, which stands a few miles from the town of Dorchester in Dorset. The central enclosure measures some 925 m (3,000 ft) in length by 524 m (1,700 ft) at its widest point, with entrances at either end. The enclosure is surrounded by three earth ramparts, open at the ends of the fort, with outworks to defend the two entrances. The inner embankment was topped by a circuit of dry-stone walling, with massive timber gates to close off the inner area.

We have no means of proving exactly how Vespasianus moved his legion to the territory of the Durotriges, but it is possible that he used present-day Chichester as a base for a marine operation and mounted the attack from the Solent. Alternatively, he could have conducted the operation completely on land, but the latter method would have totally negated any chance of surprising the Durotriges.

The actual assault on *Mai-dun* would have commenced with a steady barrage of missiles from the 'artillery' of the legion, which consisted basically of two types of *catapulta*: the *ballista*, which was in the form of an oversized crossbow, worked by two vertical twisted skeins of cord and varying considerably in size. Machines of that type could also be mounted on carts (*carroballista*), which enabled their crews to move them rapidly to points of need. The *ballista* was used to throw both wooden darts, tipped with a small iron head, and spherical stone projectiles, varying in size from

Section of the reliefs of Trajan's Column, Rome, showing a *carroballista* (left) and another *ballista* being set up on a rampart.

78

that of an orange, up to quite massive specimens about the size of a modern football; though the latter were normally used with permanently mounted machines, employed for such purposes as town or coastal defence. Such large *ballistae* were certainly to be found in use on Hadrian's Wall.

The alternative form of *catapulta* was called an *onager*, after the wild ass, because of its great 'kick' upon discharge. Those machines again varied in dimension quite considerably and were similar to the medieval mangonel in principle, being operated by a single horizontal twisted skein of rope. The *onager* was designed purely as a stone-thrower and could be built to such a size that a shot weighing between 22 to 27 kg (50 to 60 lb) could carry over a distance of 366 m (400 yd).

No doubt the lighter, quick-loading *ballistae* continued to shoot at the defenders on top of the ramparts as the legionaries began the infantry assault, in an effort to relieve the soldiers of some of the large number of sling-stones and spears which would have been hurled down upon them from the main rampart; one of the fort's 'ammunition dumps' was found to contain in the region of 20,000 sling-stones. That the *ballistae* were capable of shooting down adversaries at such distances may be evidenced by the remains of one defender; for still lodged in one of his vertebrae is the iron head of a catapult dart or 'bolt', which had entered from the front whilst still on a rising trajectory, judging by the angle at which it penetrated the man's abdomen.

The archaeological evidence clearly indicates that the hill-fort was attacked at the weaker eastern end, though one might expect that Vespasianus made a feint move towards the western entrance in order to cause the defenders to divide their force as the main assault went ahead.

The attack on the eastern gate has to be imagined, since there is no surviving ancient manuscript to provide us with such details; indeed there is no definite proof that LEGIO II AUGUSTA was the legion responsible for the storming of *Mai-dun*. However, by sheer deduction, that legion's presence has become accepted fact.

The narrow entry ways to the gates, passing between the steep embankments, meant that the legionaries would have been exposed to whatever missiles the defenders were able to bring to bear upon them; so possibly that would have been an occasion when the famous *testudo* (tortoise) formation was brought into play. The formation was taken up by raising the great legionary shields over the men's heads and overlapping them to form a series of sturdy lines, each shield supporting the next; lines of shields held vertically in their normal attitude along the front and down the sides completed the box-like defence.

Once the *testudo* had made its laborious way up to the gates, there remained the problem of effecting entry into the enclosure and it is impossible, as yet, to tell from the available evidence how this was done. If the legionaries were unable to force open the gates, they could conceivably have scaled the grass-covered final embankment and breached the dry-stone wall at the top; a hazardous undertaking, but not impossible when one considers the construction under fire of the siege ramp platform at Masada in AD 72–73.

The ensuing hand-to-hand combat was fierce and bloody; skeletal

'Scorpion' *ballista*, based on the remains of a catapult found at Ampurias in Spain. Machines of this type threw iron-tipped darts, or small stone shot.

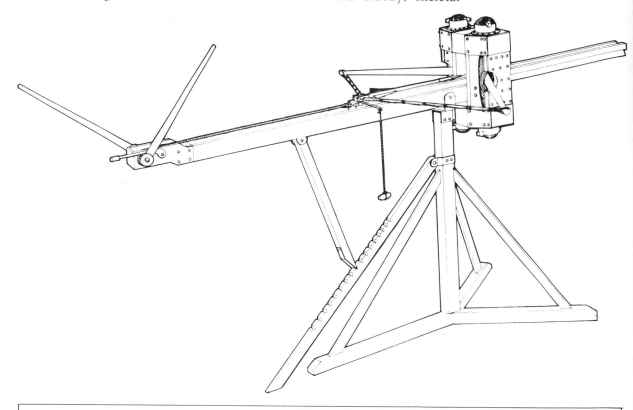

PLATE 9   A senior officer's orders are relayed by a *cornicen*. Second half of the first century AD

The officer's helmet is a unique specimen which was found at Autun, France, and now in the collection of the Musée Rolin, Autun. The piece is of gilded bronze and of Etrusco-Corinthian style, with a laminated neck-guard. The short cuirass is typical of the body armours depicted on the very many representations of provincial governors, generals and others of rank, a large number of which show the full-length cuirass with an abdominal extension. He carries a sword called a *parazonium*, an officer's dress weapon of Romano-Hellenic pattern, seldom included in statuary. The *pteruges* of an officer of this rank would doubtless have been fine white linen with gilded fringing.

The officer's mount is caparisoned with a fine set of silvered trappings based on a number of examples, clearly belonging to the same *frena* (harness), which may have once decorated the mount of Pliny the Elder, when he served as the Prefect of a cavalry regiment in Lower Germany; now in the collection of the British Museum. The author has coupled these trappings with a fine hackamore (nose-guard) which would seem to complete the balance of the harness decoration. None of the fittings from the animal's head, such as the bit and associated metals, is present in the original find of trappings from Xanten, Germany.

The *cornicen* wears a short *lorica hamata* with 'dagged' edges; the

practice of working the extremities of the mail into points, which appears to have begun during the second half of the first century AD. The great curved trumpet, *cornu*, an example of which was recovered from the ruins of *Pompeii*, was certainly used to give some signals to troops in the field. Caesar describes how a trumpet-call was used in an attempt to recall troops at *Gergovia* in Gaul in 52 BC; however, what range of signals was available, or what those signals were, remains unknown. The *cornu* was also used to provide music for gladiatorial combats, accompanied by a water organ.

remains of the defenders in shallow graves within the enclosure, now displayed in the Dorchester County Museum, Dorchester, show that well enough. But it is also sadly obvious that the Romans, for an unknown reason, committed the same kind of atrocity against the Durotriges as the world has witnessed with lamentable frequency in more modern times; neither age, nor sex, protected those hapless folk and it appears that some of the corpses were mutilated even after death.

Once the murderous assault was concluded, the Romans set about slighting the defensive stone circuit and the gates. The surviving Britons interred the pitiful remains of their comrades and relatives, placing in their graves the normal goods required in the after-life.

By AD 47, the Romans had established their presence firmly over roughly half of what is England today and Governor Plautius had reached the termination of his service in the new province; returning home no doubt well satisfied with his accomplishment since the day he landed in Kent.

He was replaced late in the year by one Publius Ostorius Scapula, who arrived to discover himself confronted by the disintegration of the order that Plautius had left behind him; Tacitus described the province as in a state of chaos. Hostile tribes, believing that the Romans would be disadvantaged by the onset of winter and the new Governor's unfamiliarity with the province, had started raiding into the occupied territory. Scapula immediately went onto the offensive with his auxiliary forces, surprising the hostiles and causing them to disperse before his rapid advance.

In an attempt to forestall further trouble, he then proposed to disarm all the tribesmen within the Roman pale, whom he considered to be disaffected. Not too surprisingly, the tribesmen had no wish to be deprived of their weapons; not only would such deprivation have engendered a feeling of being at the none too tender mercy of the Romans, but such artefacts were doubtless regarded as symbols of their manhood and prowess.

Consequently the Iceni, who had never before attempted to cause any conflict with the invaders and were indeed, up to that point, their allies, broke into open revolt, joined by the neighbouring tribes. That the Britons were unsure of their ability to confront the Roman troops in the open is shown by the fact that they chose to draw up their force within a defensive earthwork, which the historian Tacitus described as 'rustic', perhaps because it was of normal native construction and unlike the well-built Roman works. The place described may have been at Cherry Hinton, near Cambridge.

The entrance to the enclosure was very narrow and precluded the effective use of the Roman cavalry. To make full use of his force, which contained no legionaries, Scapula ordered his troopers to dismount and fight on foot, in support of the infantry cohorts. At the signal for battle, the auxiliaries burst through the earthwork and a hard fight began. The tribesmen quickly found that the protection afforded by the earth banks was no more than a trap which they had set for themselves and despite fighting for their lives with desperate courage, all was in vain.

We are not told the numbers of men involved in the action, but that it was a sufficiently sound defeat to quieten not only the Iceni, but all the other tribes within the occupied territory. With fear now thoroughly instilled, Scapula turned his attention to the Deceangli, who were wise enough not to attempt to confront the Romans openly as they pillaged their territory; instead they ambushed a Roman column on the march, but suffered defeat even by such hit-and-run tactics.

Scapula's conquest of the northern part of Wales was interrupted by yet another uprising to his rear: this time by the Brigantes, whose huge territory covered much of north Britain as far as the river Tyne and the Solway Firth. However, the suppression of their revolt seems to have been remarkably easy. Tacitus tells us briefly that the Brigantes subsided, presumably when threatened with fierce military action, and that the ringleaders were put to death; the remainder were allowed to go free. One may believe that the apparent clemency was aimed at maintaining peace with that tribe until such time as the subjugation of Wales was completed.

Immediately further trouble developed on the frontier with South Wales with the tribe of the Silures. Their continuing threat obliged Scapula to move a legionary unit, LEGIO XX VALERIA, from the new Roman capital at *Camulodunum* and establish a strong military base on the river Severn; evidence suggests that this was at Kingsholm, near Gloucester. Whether or not there was also a detachment from LEGIO II AUGUSTA present is not certain; the legion's headquarters were at Exeter at the time, but the practice of placing *vexillationes* elsewhere was quite usual. The military establishment at *Camulodunum* was replaced with a number of veteran soldiers, whose task, we are told, was to prevent the Trinovantes from breaking into rebellion and to accustom them to the rule of Roman law. Just how unwise such a policy could be became all too apparent in AD 60.

The military build-up on the Severn was probably far greater than our knowledge indicates and may have included *vexillationes* from all the three other legions, as well as a sizeable force of auxiliaries. Once Scapula was ready to move against the Silures, there re-emerges the figure of that noble and able chieftain, Caratacus. Though the hearts of the Silures were high, owing to his almost legendary presence, Caratacus avoided battle with the large Roman force, perhaps because he considered that either his numbers were too inferior, or the terrain did not suit such an engagement, and he then, in the words of Tacitus, 'moved the war into the territory of the Ordovices'. There he doubtless hoped to gain the help of that powerful tribe and that of many others of the anti-Roman faction.

Caratacus knew that if the Romans were to be driven out of Britain and the old freedoms restored, he must sooner or later destroy their military domination and he decided to engage Scapula in a major battle as he moved north in search of the massing British force. The precise site of the action is unknown, but logical interpretation of Tacitus and the existing ancient trackways lead to the suggestion that it took place close to present-day Newtown, in Powys. Tacitus tells us that there were steep hills to one side of the British position and that where the gradient was less rapid, the tribesmen had erected rough stone ramparts. To the front of the position was a river, presumably the Severn, which again the British seem to have thought would give added protection.

Scapula, with his forces drawn up on the opposing side of the river, was somewhat intimidated by the obstacles and the ferocious hordes of warriors waiting for him to dare to attack. This time it was the soldiers themselves who did not need encouragement and they clamoured for the battle to begin. Accordingly, once closer inspection of the British deployment had been made, to discover any weaknesses, Scapula led his men across the river and the legionaries began the assault on the improvised ramparts.

In that the Romans seriously underestimated the strength and determination of the defending force and they were obliged to withdraw with heavy casualties. The second assault, however, was more carefully planned and the legionaries advanced against the rampart in *testudo* formation. Under the protection of the shields, the soldiers were able to dismantle the rampart and come to close quarters with the tribesmen. Once the defences were broken through, the battle became another illustration of the futility of poorly armed and indisciplined natives attempting to combat Roman troops.

The light-armed auxiliaries hurled javelins into the disorderly mass of Britons, whilst the legionary infantry advanced in close order, driving the enemy up the incline to the hill-tops. The Romans pursued them hotly and eventually the Britons found themselves faced by legionaries on one hand and the auxiliaries on the other. Tacitus uses the word *spathae* to describe the swords of the auxiliaries, instead of *gladii*, which may suggest that Scapula was again fielding dismounted cavalry troopers, as he had done against the Iceni; for the *spatha* was very definitely a cavalry weapon, and really rather a poor one when compared with the heavier *gladius* which is always shown carried by the auxiliary infantry on their grave *stelae*.

The victory for Scapula included the capture of Caratacus' wife and daughter and the surrender of one of his brothers, whose name is not recorded; however, Tacitus wrote that the Emperor pardoned Caratacus, his wife and *brothers*, but whether or not these were brothers-in-law is not clear. No doubt to Scapula's chagrin, the most desired captive all, Caratacus, was not to be found amongst the prisoners. He had somehow managed to escape and made his way to Queen Cartimandua of the Brigantes, hoping to continue the war with her tribe's assistance. But his dreams were in vain; Cartimandua promptly had him arrested and handed over to Scapula.

So ended the career of the great warrior who had defied the might of Rome for eight years. He and his family were taken to Rome and featured in the triumphal procession of Scapula; but so famous a figure had he become and such was the courage he displayed before the Emperor that he was not executed, but was allowed to live on in Italy with his family. Scapula returned to Britain and, exhausted by his exertions, died soon afterwards.

The campaign against the Druids and the Boudican revolt

AD 60−61

Upon the premature death in AD 58 of Quintus Veranius, the military governor of Britain, whose task was to continue the westward movement of the conquest into Wales, largely against the two major warlike tribes, the Silures in the south and the Ordovices of the north, Rome appointed in his place a tough and resolute soldier, Gaius Suetonius Paullinus. The latter's previous experience of mountain warfare, which he had gained in North Africa, was probably the main reason for his appointment, since it would have well fitted him for operations against the Ordovices in particular, who inhabited the mountainous region of Snowdonia.

The northern thrust into Wales was probably the more important campaign of the two in Roman eyes, for behind the territory of the Ordovices lay the seat of Druidic power in Britain — the Isle of Anglesey (*Mona Insula*). The Druidic cult exercised a strong religious influence over the lives and attitudes of the British tribesmen, which they exploited, as religious belief has so often been exploited, for political ends. Thus Anglesey had become the focal point for resistance to the occupation and many anti-Roman Britons had moved there to seek the protection of the Druids, adding to the large number of inhabitants already living there at that time, according to the historian Tacitus, whose brief history of the events, together with that of Dio Cassius, provides the major source of our knowledge.

Unfortunately, Tacitus makes no reference to any campaign against the Silures by Paullinus; however, since Veranius had made some attempt to subdue that tribe prior to his death in AD 58, it is most likely that Paullinus had, by some measure, reduced any threat from that direction during AD 59, before moving against the north the following year.

Evidently, Paullinus chose to eliminate the Druids and their followers before attempting to overcome the Ordovices, in the belief that to destroy the religious and political power-base would make the second objective less arduous in its accomplishment.

Accordingly, the advance would have been made initially into the territory of the Deceangli, already pacified some years earlier by the Governor Ostorius Scapula, which lay to the north of the Snowdon range. The force consisted of LEGIO XIIII GEMINA and LEGIO XX VALERIA with supporting auxiliaries of unknown numbers, though one may expect that

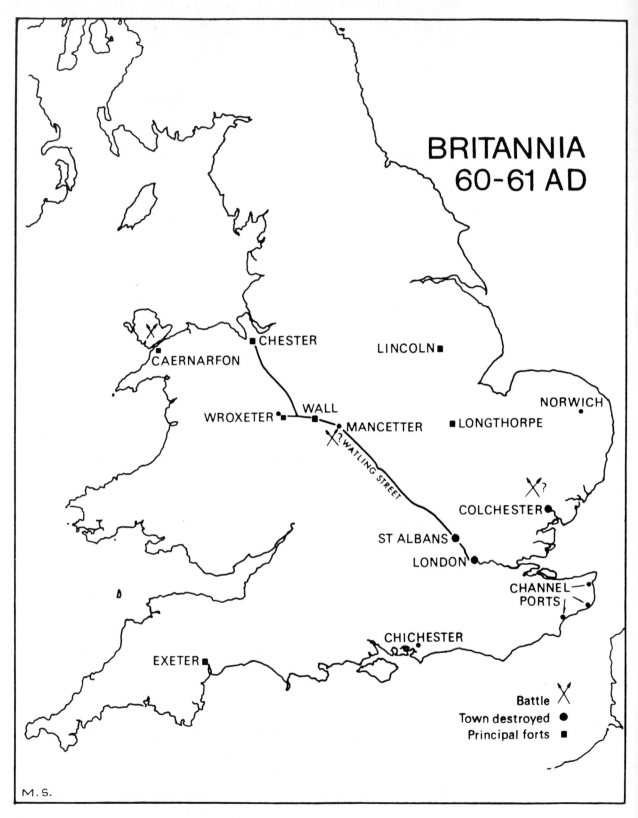

BRITANNIA
60-61 AD

CHESTER

LINCOLN

CAERNARFON

NORWICH

WALL

WROXETER   MANCETTER   LONGTHORPE

WATLING STREET

COLCHESTER

ST ALBANS

LONDON

CHANNEL
PORTS

CHICHESTER

EXETER

Battle   ✗
Town destroyed ●
Principal forts ■

M.S.

Map of Britain, AD 60–61.

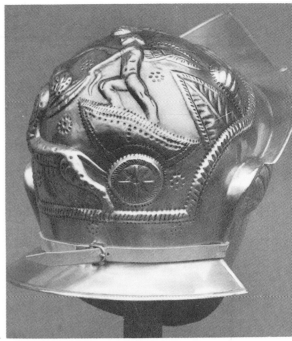

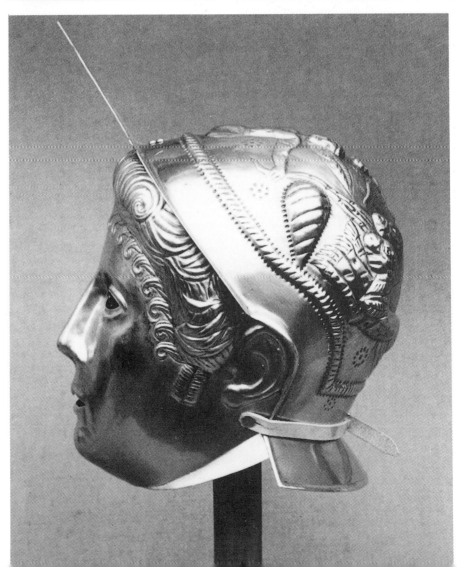

Bronze helmet skull-piece of Cavalry Sports type 'B'. Restored model by the author, drawn from the original piece from Newstead, Scotland, now in the National Museum of Antiquities of Scotland, Edinburgh. Probably manufactured during the second half of the first century AD.

the cavalry contingent was fairly large and included a unit of Batavians. A base for the operations would clearly have been constructed in that region, for at that point the campaign against the Ordovices was still in Paullinus' mind; it was probably built on the site later occupied by the great legionary fortress of Chester (*Deva*), beside the river Dee.

The advance to the Isle of Anglesey could have been made in one of two ways; either by land to the north of the Snowdon range, or by sea, or conceivably simultaneously by sea and land. To have transported the entire force from the then navigable river Dee round the coast to the Menai Strait would seem to have been a somewhat hazardous undertaking, in view of the rather inferior nature of Roman warships and troop-transports, and to attempt to navigate the treacherous narrows of the Strait itself would, for that reason, have been virtually suicidal. The loss of the training ship HMS *Conway* in 1953 was occasioned by a very slight misjudgement of the tide, the ship being driven onto the mainland shore close to where Thomas Telford's suspension bridge stands today. How much worse then for the Romans, unfamiliar with the terrain, their tiny vessels packed with men, horses, mules and tons of equipment!

The coastal corridor, though there was the likelihood of being surprised by the Ordovices and there were two rivers, the Clwyd and the Conway, to be crossed, was probably regarded as the lesser of two evils by Paullinus. Arriving at the Strait, he would doubtless have secured both the then fordable point on the Strait at Bangor and the wider, though apparently quite shallow, reach at Caernarfon. Since there is no contemporary archaeological evidence available for the disposition of Paullinus' forces,

PLATE 10   A cavalry trooper in the 'Greek' team collects a dummy javelin from his *calo* during the *hippika gymnasia*. Second half of the first century AD

The helmet is based on the famous Ribchester specimen in the British Museum. This splendid example of a cavalry 'sports' head-piece, found near the fort at Ribchester, Lancashire, England, is virtually intact. One feature which is not present on any of the other surviving specimens occurs with the ring fasteners placed either side of the skull's occiput (only one survives); the hair streamers shown to be tied to the rings are hypothetical. The trooper is wearing a *lorica hamata* under a special embroidered tunic; the mail has been included by the author because this aspect may have been arbitrary. The Roman historian Arrianus, in his work *Tactica*, states that *loricae* were not worn with the special tunics; however, it is clear that *loricae squamatae* were made specifically for this purpose, though at a later date, and since the 'game' involved the throwing of wooden javelins at troopers acting as targets, one might expect that at least the 'targets' wore some protection during the first century. The man is also shown to wear laminated bronze thigh-guards and metal greaves. An example of a thigh-guard was excavated from the fort at Newstead in Scotland, but whether or not it can be definitely identified as a piece of sports equipment, it is impossible to say. Greaves for troopers of the teams of this date are also something of a problem, since there is no known specimen belonging to this century and those shown are based on the appearance of later types. It has been suggested that such greaves may have been made from boiled leather, but as there is no surviving specimen of a centurion's greaves at all, the matter remains open to question.

The mount has a chamfron based on an example also from Newstead, made basically from hide with elaborate studded decoration and a peytral with applied figures in the collection of the Civico Museo Romano, Brescia. It is clear from finds of sports material that there were various types of horse furniture for this purpose, including eye-shields which were not attached to chamfrons, but were simply strapped in position.

one is obliged to draw upon evidence from a later period: the construction of a stone fort at *Segontium,* above and behind Caernarfon, clearly indicates that the Romans considered the locality to be a position of strength, and it was probably the site of the main camp.

Some argument exists as to precisely where the assault took place, but examination of the terrain today, which has changed little since Roman times, appears to make Caernarfon the most likely candidate. The Strait is certainly very much narrower at Bangor, but the Anglesey shore is dangerously steep and the Roman soldiers could easily have found themselves in the same disastrous position as that encountered by the American First and Twenty-Ninth Divisions on Omaha beach during the Normandy landings in June 1944, except that the Romans would have been able to withdraw.

According to Tacitus, the infantry were ferried across the Strait in flat-bottomed craft 'built to contend with the shifting shallows', which sounds much more in keeping with the sand bars at the southern end of the Strait, which were probably no less evident in ancient times than they are today. Whether or not the assault craft were built on the river Dee and then towed round the coast, or were constructed in the shelter of the river Seiont at Caernarfon, is a matter for speculation. Paullinus may have discovered the need for such craft only after his surveyors had been able to inspect the Strait at close quarters. In any event, there can be no doubt that the legionary engineers were entirely capable of undertaking the task on site.

The legionary infantry were to spearhead the attack, and because there could never have been any chance of surprising the Britons, they were faced with the unenviable prospect of effecting a landing on a beach seething with armed men. Added to that were the women, who in their black robes and with wild hair flying, brandished flaming torches. There too were the Druid priests, raising their arms to the heavens and calling down hideous curses upon the Romans.

So overawed were the soldiers by the display, that they fell into a state of virtual paralysis; they simply stood up on their boats as they neared the opposing shore and made no effort to protect themselves from the hail of missiles that fell upon them. Finally, we are told, the men's spirit returned and they exhorted each other and were urged by their general not to fear what lay before them. Here, perhaps, we are given a glimpse of the character of Paullinus, an officer, it appears, who led his men from the front: a cool soldierliness, soon to be called upon in earnest.

The tension released, the legionaries fought their way ashore. Once on land, their standards gleaming above the lines of shields and licking swordblades, the Romans drove forward and the well-trained machine began its grisly work. The Britons were massacred: either cut down by the sword, or enveloped in the flames of their own torches. A tradition persists on Anglesey to this day that a massacre took place in the fields that run down to the Strait from Porthamel Hall, opposite Caernarfon, known

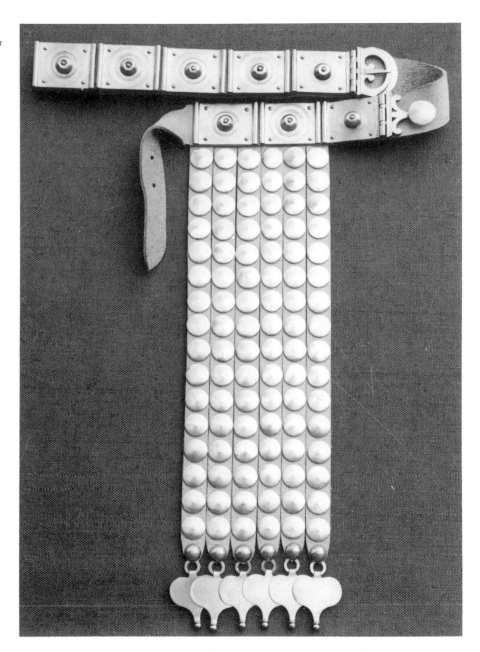

Military belt of auxiliary type. Belt fittings were almost always tinned or silvered. Author's reconstruction based on specimens from Hod Hill, Dorset, and York, England.

somewhat luridly as 'The Fields of Blood'. Whether or not the legend refers to the Roman assault on the island, nobody can be certain, though the fields in question would seem to be a very likely locale for the carnage.

The cavalry followed the infantry force, some fording the Strait while others, in deeper water, swam beside their horses, and with the Britons in retreat before the legionary onslaught no doubt pursued them and cut down as many of the survivors as they could. How long the slaughter continued, we are not told, but one may imagine that the Romans were very thorough in their task. When the blood-letting was over, they set

Reconstructed gateway of a semi-permanent fort and section of the turf and timber rampart. Lunt Fort Interpretive Centre, Coventry, England.

about the eradication of the Druidic cult centre, which was probably on the site now occupied by RAF Valley, where various Celtic objects were unearthed during the construction of the Air Force base.

Tacitus tells us, with apparent distaste, that the Druids soaked their altars in human blood and undertook divination using the viscera of their victims (the latter a practice which was to be found in the late Roman army). It is difficult to accept such criticism as genuine, in view of the known facts concerning the Romans' own highly organised cruelty, used as a means of popular entertainment, which by the first century AD had lost its original religious rationale.

Whilst Paullinus was thus engaged and probably planning his forthcoming campaign against the Ordovices, alarming dispatches reached him of a rising in the south-east of the Province. Mounting oppression by the increasing numbers of retired soldiers in particular, and probably also a large number of civil immigrants, had at last become too much for the indigenous population to bear. The tribe quoted as having suffered most at their hands was that of the Trinovantes, many of whom had been driven from their homes and lands by the normal Roman custom of awarding land grants to time-expired soldiers, which appears little better than simple theft.

Such treatment was, of course, a cause of increasing bitterness and desire for revenge, which required only a spark to ignite a terrible conflagration. The veterans were not solely responsible for the dangerous circumstances; the serving soldiers actively encouraged the brutal behaviour of their countrymen, hoping that they would enjoy the same kind of benefits at the termination of their enlistment. Added to all that malfeasance was the construction of the great new temple of the divine Claudius, being built at *Camulodunum*, the old British stronghold which the Romans had made their provincial capital; an edifice which the British naturally regarded as a symbol of Roman domination and hated accordingly.

The tribe of the Iceni, on the other hand, had fared rather better than their southern neighbours, the Trinovantes, thanks to the relationship of 'client' status which existed between their King, Prasutagus, and the Roman State, perhaps as a result of aid rendered to the Romans during the initial stages of the invasion, similarly afforded to them by King Cogidubnus of the Regni. Probably in order that those favourable relations should continue during the reign of the Emperor Nero and to secure half of his estate for his descendants, Prasutagus had devised a will which named the Emperor and his own two daughters as co-heirs to his property and wealth, which was said to be considerable. Since the King must have been well aware of the greed of the settlers and the appropriations being visited upon other tribes less fortunate than his own, the will was probably a desperate diplomatic move to stave off the rapacity of the Romans and to secure the rights and liberties of his people.

Alas, his hopes were in vain, for upon his death, which apparently occurred whilst Paullinus was engaged in the elimination of the Druids,

Bronze shield boss from LEGIO VIII AUGUSTA recovered from the river Tyne. The piece is decorated with punching, engraving, silvering and niello inlay. In the collection of the British Museum.

PLATE 11   Auxiliaries defend an artificer's depôt against an attack by Dacian warriors during Trajan's first Dacian campaign in AD 101

Slingers from the Balearic Islands had been used by the Roman army for many years and they were certainly employed during Caesar's conquest of Gaul. Whilst such methods of combat may seem rather primitive, a high degree of marksmanship can be achieved with the sling-stone and serious injuries inflicted.

Another primitive, though effective, weapon is the age-old club which has remained with mankind throughout history, in one form or another; today it is still to be found in royal regalia in the guise of the sceptre.

Archers were again an integral part of the Roman auxiliary forces, with their valuable capability of long-range effect. Arrows were a better form of dispensable weapon than the javelin, being very much cheaper to produce and having greater range. The sinew-backed bows carried by these men were of complex design and were smaller and lighter than any bow of comparable power. The sinew lamination of more recent specimens was taken from the great neck tendon of an ox and applied under tension which caused the bow to reverse its curve when unstrung; those of the Levantine *sagittarii* also had long horn tips, which have survived in some quantity. The method of loose used was the 'thumb-ring' or 'Mongolian release', effected by placing a ring of bone or ivory on the thumb of the draw-hand with the string lying in a slight depression in the ring's surface; the thumb was clenched inwards by the index finger. The helmets of these men are very distinctive in their conical form and the type shown, of which only the skull-piece is original, was probably a Roman manufacture aimed at maintaining that national identity. The neck-guard could have been constructed either from lames as shown, or a sheet of fabric with *squamae*. The long gowns of the *sagittarii* are also an obvious indication of their non-Roman origin. Few of these archers appear to have used an arm-guard or 'bracer' to prevent the bow-string striking the forearm, a most painful experience! However, because of the section of the bow's grip, it is possible to allow the bow to revolve slightly upon loosing, thus preventing what would otherwise be considerable injury over a number of looses.

representatives of the *Procurator*, Decianus Catus, possibly in accordance with instructions from Rome, entered the territory of the Iceni and began virtually to pillage not only the Royal household, but the estates of the Icenian nobles as well, reducing them to the status of slaves.

Official Roman policy or not, such behaviour was regarded as intolerable by the Iceni, who were unaccustomed to being treated as a conquered people. The late King's widow, Boudica, understandably, if unwisely, protested, but was simply met with violence against her person, being scourged, to which indignity was added sexual assault on her two young daughters.

The new order of affairs was thus driven home with inescapable clarity and the Iceni, in the no doubt justifiable belief that their tribe would soon be subjected to the same appropriations of land and property, joined with the Trinovantes and others in open revolt. The rising, according to Tacitus, had been planned for some time, at least by the Trinovantes, for it would obviously have been prudent for the insurrection to commence at a time when the major part of the occupation forces were as far distant as Roman territorial conquest would permit. Whether those intentions were in the Icenian mind prior to their loss of client status is not known; but the savage treatment of the royal family and the nobles certainly placed that tribe in the forefront of the revolt.

Queen Boudica appears from the history of Dio Cassius as a truly fearsome character, tall with tawny hair which fell to her waist, eyes of terrible glance, and harsh-voiced. As she was of royal lineage and cut such an impressive figure, especially when mounted in her war chariot, the British could not have asked for anyone finer to embody their hopes and she emerged as the overall leader. Her forces were not, of course, of the kind likely to accept the rigorous discipline necessary to make them a match for the imperial Roman military, but some degree of strategy was used at the outset of the rebellion, which must have required a measure of obedience, to have achieved success.

Predictably, the first target for their vengeance was *Camulodunum*, with its monstrous temple. However, quite some time elapsed before the British began their move against the town, sufficient for news of the uprising to reach the commander of LEGIO IX HISPANA, part of which was stationed at Longthorpe, near Peterborough, whilst a number of the legion's cohorts had been sent north to garrison the fort at Lincoln, on the frontier. The commander, Quintus Petillius Cerialis, may have underestimated the scale of the revolt, or quite possibly did not believe the Britons capable of opposing his force in the field. He was probably endeavouring to interpose himself between Boudica and *Camulodunum*, when disaster struck his expedition. The legionary infantry, probably four cohorts, were surrounded and completely destroyed. One may surmise that the Romans were ambushed while on the march, always a serious disadvantage to infantry trained to fight in an orderly and prepared manner, unused to guerrilla tactics and burdened with kit-poles, cloaks and shield-covers.

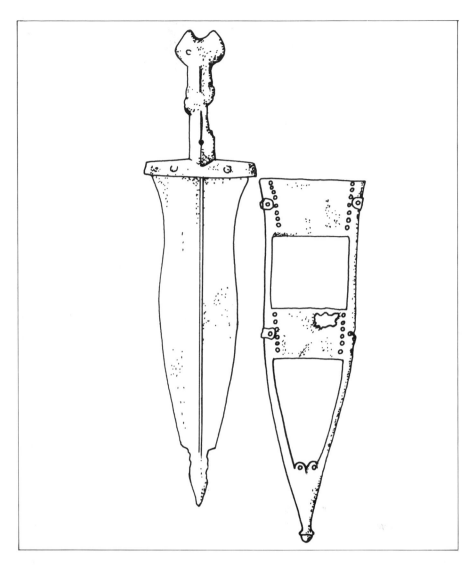

Iron dagger and iron scabbard frame found at Copthall Court, London. A hoard of similar weapons was found at Kastell Künzing, Germany, possibly the sidearms of the infantry section of a *cohors equitata*. These large rough weapons probably date from the third century AD.

Cerealis himself was fortunate enough to be able to break out with his cavalry and escaped the slaughter, returning to his camp (presumably Longthorpe), to find shelter behind its defences.

With the defeat of Cerealis, nothing now stood between Boudica and *Camulodunum*. Portents of the coming overthrow of the town helped to induce a state of terror amongst the settlers. Without any apparent cause, the statue of Victory in the town toppled over, falling face down as though in retreat. Women chanted of impending doom and told of unearthly cries and shrieks, heard both in the Senate-house and the theatre; a vision of a ruined town had been seen at the Thames estuary and the sea had turned blood-red, the tide leaving strange shapes, as of corpses, on the beaches.

One cannot be sure if those reported manifestations were invented by Tacitus for the benefit of his audience, or by the Britons in order to cause panic and lower morale. Tacitus, however, is at pains to point out that the

British were operating an effective 'fifth column' within the town, which managed to persuade the settlers that there was no need to refurbish the old legionary fortifications, which had either been slighted or allowed to fall into disrepair when the garrison was ordered out for duty further west. Evidently the settlers were uneasy enough to appeal to the *Procurator*, who was in *Londinium* (London), for assistance, to augment the small town guard, which more properly could be regarded as a police force, already *in situ*. Catus could only manage to dispatch 200 auxiliaries to their aid and even these were not completely armed.

At last the rebels surrounded the town and a desperate struggle began. No doubt the veteran soldiers did their best to resist the repeated onslaughts and accounted for many of their adversaries, but at last, hopelessly outnumbered and with the town blazing around them, they retreated to the only defensive position that remained, the great temple of Claudius. Despite their overwhelming numbers, it took a further two days before the rebels broke into the enclosure, which speaks well of the determination of the defenders. The temple itself (the platform of which is still in existence beneath the keep of the later Norman Castle), was full of non-combatants, whom the Romans had neglected to evacuate. The rebels fired the building, presumably by scaling the walls and igniting the roof timbers. Those who managed to escape the flames fared even worse, for the Britons took no prisoners and hideous deeds of torture and mutilation were their fate, especially the womenfolk: Dio Cassius wrote:

'They hung up naked the noblest and most distinguished women, then cut off their breasts and sewed them to their mouths, so that they should appear to be eating them; afterwards they impaled the victims on skewers run lengthwise through the body.'

Whilst such grotesque acts were probably performed as a barbaric religious ritual, or at least that is the excuse, one may believe that they were a cause of even greater violence towards the rebels and their sympathisers during the aftermath of the revolt.

Governor Paullinus, doubtless informed of the defeat of Cerealis, realised the very serious nature of the rebellion and decided to appraise the situation in person. Taking with him a force of cavalry, he set out for the town of *Londinium*, leaving orders for the infantry to follow on. He also dispatched messengers to the headquarters of LEGIO II AUGUSTA at Exeter (*Isca Dumnoniorum*), ordering that legion to link up with LEGIONES XIIII and XX.

As the rebels were busily engaged in their celebrations and bestialities after the fall of *Camulodunum*, Paullinus managed to reach *Londinium* in safety. Initially, he considered the possibility of saving the town, which must mean that he had not ordered his legions to concentrate in the Midlands at the time; however, after due consideration, he realised that his numbers were too few to give battle to Boudica at *Londinium*, a view reinforced by the fate of the Cerealis expedition, and he decided to abandon *Londinium* to the rebels, whilst he returned to rejoin his army in

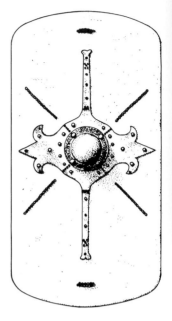

Reconstruction of an auxiliary infantry shield, based on remains found at Doncaster, Yorkshire, England. The shield board was made of a triple ply of oak and elder, faced with hide. There may also have been a painted design on the face. The shield dates from the second half of the first century AD.

Right:
Reconstruction of the *gladius* found on the site of the fort of *Segontium* near Caernarfon in Wales. The blade is of unusual form and the scabbard may have been made from thin iron sheet, of which only traces remained when the sword was discovered.

Far right:
Two cavalry swords (*spathae*) found in a grave at Canterbury, England. Both swords are of second-century date and have bronze scabbard chapes. There do not appear to have been any other scabbard mounts.

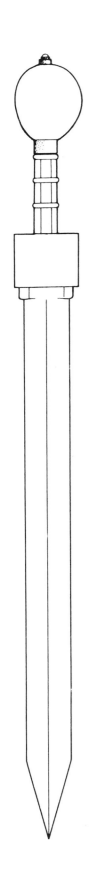
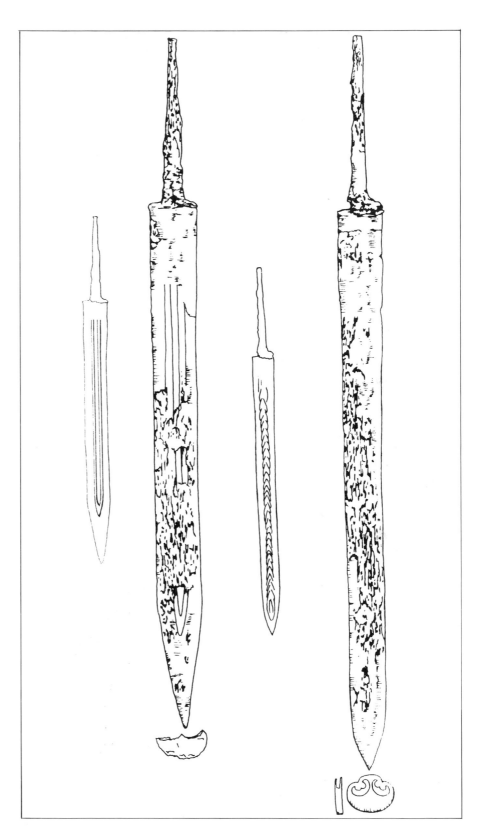

the north-west. Those of the inhabitants who wished to do so were permitted to accompany him; others probably fled southward to seek the protection of King Cogidubnus of the Regni. Ignoring appeals from those who remained in the town, Paullinus and his cavalry mounted up and clattered out along what is now the Edgware Road, perhaps wondering if they would be able to escape before Boudica cut the road north.

Fortune was with Paullinus, and he succeeded in making his way through the disaffected territory, presumably evacuating as many of the townsfolk of *Verulamium* (St Albans) as possible, for he clearly intended to sacrifice that town as well.

The rebels, in the meantime, had reached *Londinium* and the town suffered the same dreadful fate as the capital; it was razed to the ground and such inhabitants as were still there, largely old men and women, perished under the bloody hands of Boudica's warriors. A number of skulls recovered from the Walbrook stream-bed, devoid of other skeletal remains, may possibly date from that time.

Whatever concerted military plan Boudica and her more senior adherents may have had at the outset of the revolt had probably disappeared in

Elaborately decorated bronze boss from a flat oval shield (*clipeus*). The piece was probably used for the *hippika gymnasia*, cavalry sports. In the collection of the Städtisches Museum, Wiesbaden.

the tide of bloodshed and looting, for we are told by Tacitus that the natives thought only of plunder and made for places where most could be gained without opposition, by-passing all military installations.

Verulamium was the next and last major town to be destroyed in the uprising. Like the other two, it had no permanent defences at that time; those which can be seen today date from the Hadrianic period. Deaths at the three towns were estimated at 70,000, both Romans and provincials; but in view of the relatively small size of the places involved and the fact that a great many of the people must have fled before destruction was visited upon them, the figure seems rather exaggerated. However, if one takes into account all the rural dwellings, such as the farming communities, which were no doubt overrun, the figure may not be too far from the truth.

On reaching his main force, perhaps near Wall (*Letocetum*), close to Lichfield in Staffordshire, Paullinus was greeted with news that was as unexpected as it was unwelcome; the sorely needed assistance from LEGIO II AUGUSTA had not arrived. At the time the orders had reached that legion's headquarters, both the commander and his senior tribune were absent, the command being left, as was customary, under the charge of the *Praefectus castrorum*, one Poenius Postumus. That a direct order from the Governor should have been disobeyed by a Camp Prefect was, of course, an extremely serious breach of regulations and it is difficult to postulate precisely what could have caused his disobedience; in a man who had risen to hold that office, cowardice appears as an impossibility. Ultimately, upon hearing of the victory won by Paullinus, he was overcome with shame, according to Tacitus, and took his own life. Under the circumstances, he

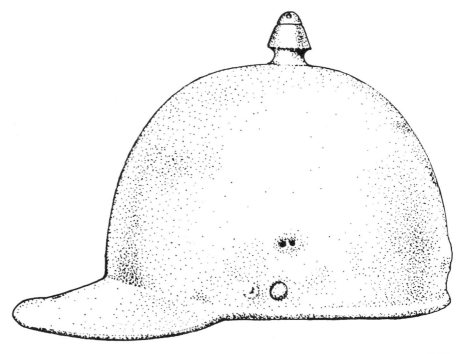

Bronze infantry helmet skull of Coolus type 'E', found at St Albans, Hertfordshire, England. This skull-piece, which originally had cheek-guards and a peak, also has a hollow brow edge, an unusual feature. Probably made in the early first century AD. In the collection of the Verulamium Museum, St Albans.

would certainly have been disgraced, if not executed for his refusal; so perhaps he simply pre-empted a miserable end.

Paullinus was thus deprived of some two to three thousand legionary infantry and probably a large number of auxiliaries as well, which meant that his total force must have numbered between 12,000 to 15,000 all told, depending upon how many auxiliaries he was able to pull back from the frontier forts without inviting another uprising from the north. One may imagine that in such an emergency, personnel whose duties were normally non-combatant would have been employed as additional infantry.

Intelligence regarding the size of Boudica's force must have made it very clear to Paullinus that he would be totally unable to defeat the rebels by

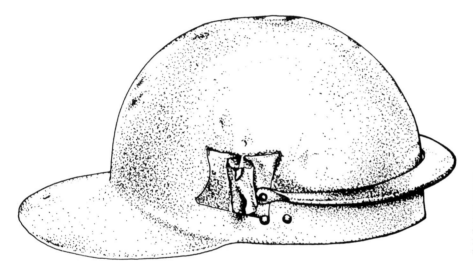

Bronze infantry helmet skull of Coolus type 'E', found in the Walbrook streambed, London. The helmet would originally have been fitted with cheek-guards and a crest-spike. Probably made in the early first century AD. In the collection of the British Museum.

PLATE 12   An auxiliary cavalryman raises the alarm at a turret on Hadrian's Wall. Second quarter of the second century AD

The *sagittarii* shown in this illustration belong to I HAMIORUM SAGITTARIORUM. A corps of these men were stationed at Carvoran on the Wall at the end of the reign of Hadrian. The equipment is based on a grave *stela* which was found at the Housesteads Fort and is now in the collection of the Museum of Antiquities, Newcastle upon Tyne, England. The helmet is copied from a fine example found at Bryastovets in Bulgaria, now in the collection of the Archaeological Museum, Sofia. The helmet is of embossed bronze with a tinned background to accentuate the relief. The conical helmets were also made of iron, a fact attested by the

remains of a pair of iron cheek-guards which were found inside the cavalry helmet skull-piece from the fort at Northwich; clearly the helmet skull was being used as a receptacle for odd items which were not in use, a common habit in workshops which unfortunately tends to confuse the modern archaeologist! Unlike other Levantine *sagittarii*, this archer is shown to wear a short tunic; the *lorica hamata* is presumed. He has a waist-belt with a long knife and carries a small hatchet.

The cavalry trooper's helmet is of Auxiliary Cavalry type 'E'. These massive iron head-pieces with conical rivets securing the skull

reinforces appeared late in the first century AD and certainly remained in use up to the middle years of the second century, no doubt for as long as they were serviceable. He is shown to wear a hauberk with a cape shoulder-doubling. Whilst it would be true to say that a large number of the cavalry of the time wore no doubling at all, it is quite likely that many of the older style were still to be found in the early second century. Whether or not cavalry units of this period still carried quivers of light javelins is not certain; however, the likelihood should not be dismissed.

using normal Roman battle deployment and there his resourceful mind came to the fore. In that he was no doubt aided by the amount of time the slow-moving mass of insurgents allowed him to choose the ground upon which his tiny force was to make its stand.

He selected a defensive position in a narrow defile, heavily wooded at the rear. In that way he presented only a short front, which prevented the enemy from bringing large numbers to bear at any one time and eliminated any fear of being surrounded. Of course, the woods at his rear did mean that retreat would have been very difficult, if not impossible; but under the circumstances, there was no alternative: the Romans would either conquer or perish.

The actual site of the battle remains unknown; however, by logical deduction, one distinct possibility is at present-day Mancetter (Roman *Manduessedum*, which name means 'the place of the chariots'), where the topography bears a reasonable resemblance to that described by Tacitus.

The Romans, drawn up in their defile, watched as the masses of British cavalry and infantry bands poured onto the plain in front of them, followed by wagons and carts laden with booty from the sacked towns. The warriors also brought with them their women and children, in order that they might enjoy the spectacle of the massacre of the Roman overlords. These they stationed in a great semi-circle at their rear, using the wagons as a makeshift amphitheatre.

'Their numbers were unprecedented...' wrote Tacitus, and it was said that if the Roman line had been stretched out one man deep, it would not have reached far enough. A modern estimate of British strength is in the region of 100,000, though according to the Romans, the ranks contained many women. As was their custom, the British had war chariots accompanying their forces, which no doubt drove furiously up and down the Roman front, hurling insults and javelins at the stony-faced soldiers, safe in their orderly ranks behind a wall of shields.

The ancient writers tell very little about the progress of the battle that is of value to modern historians, only that the Romans kept to their defile and met the charging tribesmen with showers of their deadly javelins. The legionaries then broke out in wedge formation, with the auxiliaries in support, the archers shooting down the chariots. The latter seems to have a ring of truth, for large targets like the chariot ponies would have been an easy prey for the bowmen.

One surmises that the battle was a far longer affair than is suggested by Tacitus, and the Romans probably had to contend with numerous waves of attackers before they could begin their advance from the defile; but once the morale of the Britons began to fail in face of the steady discipline of the Romans, the elation caused by their easy past successes against old men and helpless civilians deserted them and the initiative passed to Paullinus.

Finally, the tribesmen broke and began to retreat, only to find their hopes of flight thwarted by the ring of wagons, packed with the non-combatants. The pursuing Romans seem to have developed 'battle-

Tablet of LEGIO II AUGUSTA from Benwell on Hadrian's Wall, showing the legion's Zodiac sign, Capricorn; a *vexillum* or flag standard with a triple-pronged shoe; and the legion's badge, Pegasus.

madness': not only humans, but even the baggage animals swelled the heaps of corpses.

The Romans claimed to have killed about 80,000 Britons that day; their own casualties were stated to be 400 fatalities and a slightly larger number of wounded. As with so many claims of the kind, the actual numbers were probably rather different; however, since the Roman soldier was so far superior in both training and equipment, a considerable disparity was bound to be the result.

The Romans no longer saw any serious threat and the whole army united to stamp out the remaining sparks of the rebellion that had come so close to success. A further 2,000 legionary infantry were transferred from the Rhine to replace the losses suffered by LEGIO IX HISPANA, as well as cohorts of auxiliary infantry and a cavalry wing.

Paullinus, anxious to exact swift retribution, kept the army in the field, even though the campaigning season was over and winter was approaching. Though in a sorry state, as their failure to plant crops had reduced them to starvation, the Britons remained sullen, or even openly hostile. Paullinus showed no mercy and all who exhibited the slightest signs of opposition were put to the sword and their property burned.

It seemed as though the province would never have peace, as long as Paullinus held the post of Governor. Such was the view of the new *Procurator*, Gaius Julius Alpinus Classicianus, appointed as the replacement

105

for Decianus Catus, who had fled to the Continent in the early days of the rebellion. Classicianus advised the tribes to wait until a new Governor arrived, one who would heal the wounds of the revolt, instead of inflaming them.

Eventually an excuse was found to have Paullinus removed, a minor marine disaster; but it was probably his failure to conclude peace in the province that was the main reason for his recall. Whilst the replacement of the Governor must appear as a most sensible action on the part of the central government, for a province that was in a state of turmoil was of little or no use to the Imperial revenue, there can be no doubt that it was his brilliant and decisive leadership that saved the province from even greater horrors and the re-establishment of barbarism. Paullinus stands as another clear example of a great warrior whose talents found few sympathetic ears in peacetime.

As for the sadly wronged Icenian Queen, she still rides her mighty war chariot by Westminster Bridge in London, the plinth of the monument bearing the consoling inscription 'Regions Caesar never knew thy posterity shall sway'.

Masada
AD 72–73

With the fall of Jerusalem in AD 70, after a protracted siege, Rome appointed a new military governor, Lucilius Bassus, whose task was to undertake the 'mopping-up' operations in Judaea. Bassus succeeded in reducing two major fortresses, at *Herodium* and *Machaerus*, which were still held by the Zealot insurgents, or *sicarii* as the Romans called them: a derogatory name meaning 'murderers', derived from the curved dagger which they carried called a *sica*, considered by the Romans to be an assassin's weapon. Despite those Roman successes, 3,000 of the Jews, those that had escaped from Jerusalem and *Machaerus*, began massing in the Forest of Jardes. Bassus immediately marched to the place and surrounded it with his cavalry to prevent any escape. The Jews re-

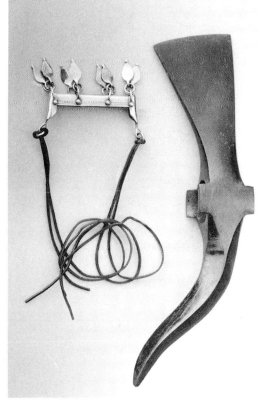

Military pickaxe (*dolabra*) and decorated sheath. The sheaths were sometimes decorated with blue beads, instead of terminals. Author's reconstruction.

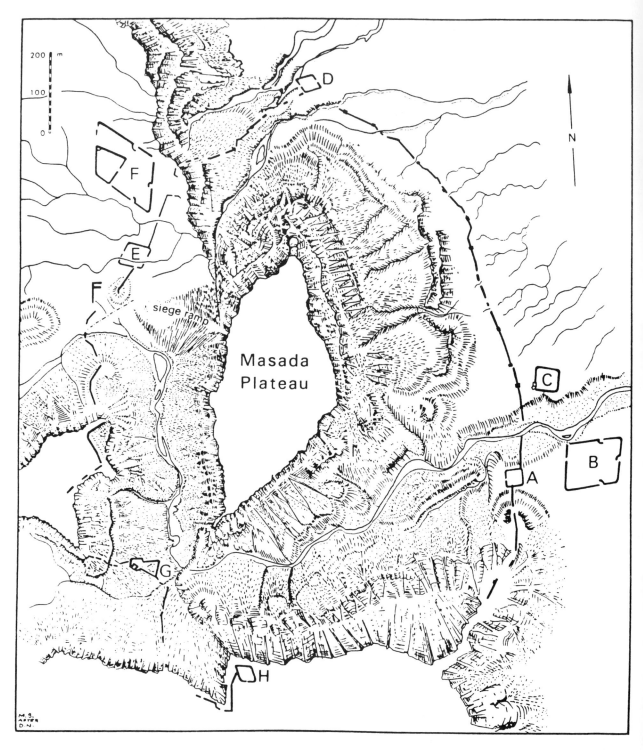

200 m
100
0

N

D

F

E

F

siege ramp

Masada
Plateau

C

B

A

G

H

M.S.
AFTER
D.N.

Plan of Masada.
A   small guard camp
B   half legion camp
C   small guard camp
D   small guard camp

E   small guard camp
F   commander's camp, half
     legion size
G   small guard camp
H   small guard camp overlooking
     the plateau

mained in what was presumably the dense cover of the trees, until Bassus ordered his legionaries to cut down the trees to expose them. Seeing the determination of the Romans, the cornered insurgents rushed out of the forest with loud cries and attacked the force surrounding them in an attempt to get away. The ensuing battle was both lengthy and hard-fought; the Jews, probably expecting to be killed anyway, found great strength in despair. But even so, not one of their number survived the action, whereas the Romans lost only twelve dead and a small number of wounded.

Bassus did not live to complete his mission and was replaced in AD 72 by Flavius Silva. The whole of Judaea had been pacified by that time, except for one pocket of resistance, the fortress of *Masada*, near Ein-Gedi by the Dead Sea. To that desolate place, which had been in rebel hands since the

Section of the reliefs of Trajan's Column, Rome, showing legionaries on the march with helmets slung from their shoulder-guards. In the foreground, another legionary fells a tree with his *dolabra*.

beginning of the war, when the small Roman garrison had been wiped out, a Zealot leader called Eleazar ben Ya'ir had taken a band of his followers and their wives and children, making a total number of 960 souls on the great rock.

The fortress, more properly a fortified plateau, of *Masada* seemed a place of unassailable safety. Built by King Herod the Great between 37 and 31 BC as part of his defences against the ambitions of Queen Cleopatra of Egypt, the rock had huge water cisterns cut into its sides, furnishing defenders with an almost inexhaustible supply of water. Apart from large storehouses where an abundance of provisions were stored, the soil of the plateau was rich and so food could also be grown in plenty without recourse to the outside world.

These factors meant that the only way in which the fortress could be reduced was by direct assault and the manner in which this was accomplished by the Romans is described in accurate detail by the Jewish historian Flavius Josephus, once a Zealot commander himself, who had defected to the Romans after the fall of the town of *Jotapata* in July of AD 67. His surviving work on the first Jewish War contains many interesting details about the Roman army and its practices.

Once established on *Masada*, Eleazar and his men used the fortress as a base from which they struck out against the surrounding country, looting and burning. According to Josephus, they had no qualms about pillaging their own countrymen, thinking it to be no more than they deserved for submitting to Roman domination. With such a state of affairs existing in

PLATE 13   An infantryman from the eastern legions attempts to save the life of a trooper from a *cohors equitata* during Trajan's second Dacian campaign, AD 105

The helmet of the cavalry trooper is based on a skull-piece from Kalkar-Hoenepel in a private German collection and a pair of cheek-guards from Königshofen near Strasbourg. In their basic form, these helmets obviously similar to the trooper's helmet in the preceding plate; however, since they were made from bronze and lack all the applied decorative plates of type 'E', this class of head-piece, denoted Auxiliary Cavalry type 'F', is considered to have belonged to the troopers of a mixed infantry and cavalry auxiliary unit called a *cohors equitata*. He carries a *spatha* with a scabbard based on two specimens found in a grave at Canterbury. Since there was no sign of any metal mounts at the throat of the

scabbards, it must be assumed that they were made of perishable material at that point, with only the chape made from bronze. The hilts of both weapons had completely disappeared and may have been stripped off prior to burial, since there was no securing terminal attached to either weapon's tang.

The legionary wears an iron helmet of Imperial Italic type 'G', based on a specimen from Israel, in the collection of the Israel Museum, Jerusalem. Helmets with similar crossed reinforces over the skull of these pieces are to be clearly seen represented on the metopes of the *Tropaeum Trajani* at Adamklissi, near the eastern end of the Danube. The reliefs of that monument also depict another feature of legionary

equipment thus far unknown in the western legions: the laminated arm-guard. These defences, so well known from gladiatorial representations, have long posed a problem to the armourer, in that they appear to have no couter plate at the elbow; however, a single rough sculpture from Chester, Cheshire, England, now in the Saffron Walden Museum, appears to attempt to portray such a plate at the elbow of the *manica* of a *retiarius* (net man). Without a couter, the flexibility of the *manica* is very severely restricted and though couters are not shown on the legionaries of the Adamklissi monument, their original presence is suspected.

the south of Judaea, there clearly could be no absolute conclusion to the Jewish war as long as that nest of rebels posed a threat to law and order and there was every possibility that the Zealots might cause more serious trouble at a later date.

The region in which *Masada* stands was, and still is, subject to extremely

Section of the reliefs of Trajan's Column, Rome, showing auxiliary cavalry and infantry. Behind them, legionaries carrying bundles of material enter the camp. A gateway is clearly shown on the right.

hot weather conditions during the summer, and one assumes therefore that Silva did not move against the fortress until the autumn of AD 72, when the worst of the heat had abated. The force which he employed for the operation consisted of LEGIO X FRETENSIS and auxiliaries of strength equal to the legion. Added to the Roman military arm, there were also thousands of Jewish prisoners, pressed into service for the duration of the siege; though Josephus makes little mention of those unfortunates.

With a total complement in the region of 15,000 and operating in an area where there was no source of water, food or timber, Silva was faced with an immense logistical problem, the solution to which was certainly one of the uses he made of the prisoners, who were forced to carry from a considerable distance as many of the supplies as possible. Heavier items, such as timber baulks and sheet iron, were probably packed in by mule.

Once the problems of supply were overcome, Silva set about the prosecution of the siege. One may imagine what a daunting prospect it was for the commander and his legionary engineers, as they surveyed the heights of the rock, with the defenders closely watching them. The first task was to seal off the fortress, so that none should escape; in order to effect that aim, along the low-lying plain to the east a continuous wall with guard towers at intervals of 73 to 91 m (80 to 100 yd) was erected, with shorter sections along the remainder of the perimeter at vulnerable points. The troops were accommodated in two half-legion camps, with interclavicular entrances, and six others of varying dimensions placed on the wall or circumvallation. All the camps and the intervening walls were constructed from rubble and appear to have been about 1.8 m (6.0 ft) in height.

Within the camp enclosures, low rubble walls were built as bases for the leather tents, which gave more headroom and ventilation, welcome improvements to the normally cramped leather tents, which would have been stiflingly hot in that region, even late in the year. But even so, the experience of modern excavators working during 1963–65 on the site proved that the winters were also most inclement, with fierce windstorms and torrential, if infrequent rain, which would have made the soldiers' lives more than a little uncomfortable.

The only means of access to the fortress plateau was by narrow winding pathways, which were not only extremely dangerous to negotiate under normal circumstances, but would have been very easily defended from the summit (a group of twelve stones, each weighing about 45 kg [100 lb], was found strategically placed above the 'Snake Path'). Thus it was necessary for Silva to devise his own way of reaching the plateau and the only course open was the construction of a massive assault ramp.

Inspection of the site revealed that there was a large outcrop, called the White Cliff, on the western side, running a long way out from the scree deposit of the main rock. Even with this advantage, there remained a height of about 137 m (450 ft) to the plateau itself. The legionaries were set to work to build the ramp on top of the White Cliff and according to Josephus, 'they fell to that work with alacrity, and abundance of them together, the bank was raised and became solid for 200 cubits' (91.5 m or 300 ft). Those few words seem to make light of the immense amount of work involved in the construction of the ramp; many long hours of sweat and blood, coupled with no one knows how many deaths caused by stones hurled down upon the toiling soldiers and probably the Jewish prisoners as well.

The ramp was secured internally with timber baulks to prevent it from collapsing and some of those timbers may be seen today, protruding from the northern side. Even when the great bank had been completed, there remained some 46 m (150 ft) to be raised before the summit could be brought under fire from the *catapultae*, shooting upwards at a high angle. That final stage of the ramp was probably a cause of a greater number of casualties than the main structure, for it consisted of a massive platform about 29 m (75 ft) in both height and breadth, built from great stones compacted together (this has long since collapsed). Whilst as much of the work as possible would have been carried out under the shelter of mantlets, the position remained a badly exposed one, without any covering fire from the *catapultae*.

The last stretch of 17 m (55 ft) was to be covered by an iron-clad timber tower, 27 m (90 ft) high, itself equipped with quick-loading *ballistae* and a ram to breach the casemate wall of the fortress. One assumes that the tower was prefabricated as much as possible before being erected on top of the platform; it certainly could not have been moved to its final position in one piece. However, this time there was a measure of protection for the engineers engaged in its construction, since large *catapultae* had already been raised onto the platform before work on the tower commenced, and again it would have been possible for the soldiers to work under the cover of a mantlet, erected against missiles from the no doubt increasingly desperate defenders above them.

As the fearsome tower rose and eventually over-topped the wall, the *ballistae* inside the structure subjected the Jews to a barrage of stone shot

Section of the reliefs of Trajan's Column, showing legionaries engaged in camp construction.

114

DATORIQVIETIS

Section of the triumphal frieze from the Forum of Trajan, incorporated into the Arch of Constantine. The Emperor is shown flanked by Mars and Victory. The figure of *Victoria* originally held a wreath over the Emperor's head and a palm branch in her left hand.

and bolts, which forced them to abandon the wall and drove them under cover. Whilst this was in progress, the ram went into action and the casemate was soon breached, but the Romans found to their surprise that the defenders had constructed another wall behind the inner casemate. The new barrier was of an ingenious construction which completely defeated the efforts of the ram. Large beams, stripped from the fortress buildings, had been laid in two parallel rows to form a double wall, with the timbers fastened together at the ends. Between the two walls, a space was left and filled with earth as a cushion to absorb the shock of the ram. To prevent the walls being shaken apart, other timbers were laid transversely across the long beams and presumably firmly attached to them.

Repeated blows from the ram only served to compress the earth packing more solidly; but the Roman commander was not to be outwitted and ordered his men to fire the structure, which, being built from dry timbers, was soon fiercely ablaze. As the fire took hold, a strong wind from the north suddenly blew the flames towards the Roman tower, which threw the men upon it into something approaching panic, for the fire nearly set the tower and the *ballistae* alight. Fortunately for them, the wind abruptly changed direction to the south and fanned the burning wall into an inferno.

The Romans were greatly cheered by that event and decided to leave the fire to destroy the defences overnight; their force, which had doubtless been waiting to begin the attack once the wall was breached, returned to camp, expecting to carry out their design the following morning.

For the Zealot leader, the sight of the blazing wall signalled the end of months of waiting and watching. Knowing full well that they had no chance of beating off the coming assault, he called together his closest comrades and told them that he considered the defeats and destruction which their people and country had suffered were the will of God; no less their own predicament, citing the change in the wind which had blown the fire against their defences as clear proof of God's desire for vengeance against the Zealots, in retribution for the many fearful things they had committed against their own countrymen during the course of the war.

He therefore entreated his followers to join him in a mass suicide pact, as a penance to God, rather than submit to the abominable treatment he knew they would receive at the hands of their conquerors. He proposed to burn the fortress and all their possessions, so that the Romans would not only find none to abuse or enslave, but nothing left to carry off as prizes of

PLATE 14   The *centurio* and infantrymen of a *cohors* with a Celtic prisoner. Hadrian's Wall, Britain, second century AD

Auxiliary units were commanded by Roman officers and the *centurio* shown here carries an oval shield, instead of the *scutum* carried by his legionary counterpart. He wears a short muscled cuirass over an arming doublet with lappets more reminiscent of senior officers of earlier days. An Imperial Gallic type 'J' iron helmet, though probably made during the latter years of the first century AD, could easily have still been in service in the middle years of the second century. He still carries the *vitis* as a symbol of his rank and right to inflict corporal punishment.

The auxiliary infantryman wears a sturdy bronze helmet of Auxiliary Infantry type 'B', based on a complete specimen recovered from the river Rhine at Mainz, in the collection of the Mittelrheinisches Landesmuseum, Mainz, Germany. Again, this helmet was made during the first century AD, but particularly because of the type of metal from which it is made, has survived into the second century. He wears a simple *lorica hamata* with 'dagged' extremities and no waist-belt or dagger. The *gladii* carried by such men were declining in quality against those of their forerunners of the first century AD.

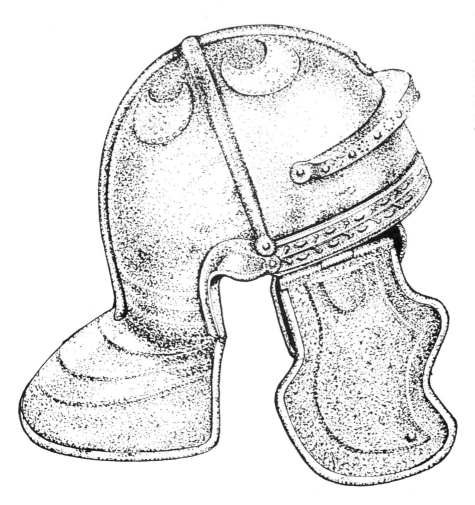

Iron infantry helmet of Imperial Italic type 'G', said to have been found in a cave at Hebron, Israel. The helmet probably dates from the late first to early second century AD. Helmets of this type are clearly depicted on the metopes of the *Tropaeum Trajani* at Adamklissi. In the collection of the Israel Museum, Jerusalem.

war. Only their food supplies were to be left intact, to prove that they had died by their own resolve and not through want of the necessities of life.

His speech was met with rapturous agreement by some, but with tears and pity for their families by others. Eleazar, seeing that all might be moved to reject his design, launched into a long speech, at first reproachful, but eventually persuasive, which included the now famous lines 'Come, while our hands are free and can hold a sword, let them do a noble service. Let us die unenslaved by our enemies and leave this world as free men in company with our wives and children.'

Eleazar had not finished speaking when those he was addressing stopped him, being much moved by his words, and made straightaway to do his bidding. Once almost all had died, the tragedy of so many deaths impressed itself upon the Zealots and they too prepared to leave this world. They set fire to all their possessions and selected by lot ten men, who were to kill the rest and one of them to dispatch the other nine. When all was done and the last man thought that no living soul was left, he set fire to Herod's palace, stood close to his family and drove his sword into his body.

118

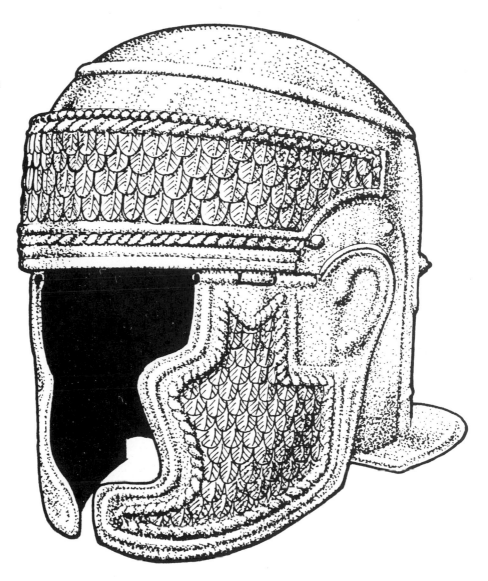

Reconstruction of a cavalry helmet from Butzbach, Germany. The feather pattern is of Thracian origin. The piece was probably made during the third quarter of the first century AD. In the collection of the Darmstadt Museum.

However, before the suicide began, two women had determined to remain alive and had taken five children with them into the water ducts of the rock, unbeknown to anyone.

At dawn the following day, the Romans burst into the fortress, fully expecting to be assailed by the Zealots. But all that confronted them was a terrible silence and smoke drifting from the palace. They stood perplexed by the strange circumstances. At length, they shouted, as though at the beginning of a battle, hoping to bring the enemy out of hiding; but none came, save for the two women, who told them what had transpired the night before. At first, the Romans could not believe the awful truth, but on breaking into the palace, they discovered the bodies. They found no joy in their having overcome such resolve, but rather admired their courage in the face of death.

Though Silva left a garrison on the rock, some of the bodies were left where they had fallen. Modern excavations in the bath-house revealed the skeletal remains of a man, no doubt a warrior, a woman and a child, most probably his family. Other remains seem to have been deposited in a cave on the side of the rock at a later date. There were found the bones belonging to twenty-five men, women and children, in a state of complete disarray, which must indicate that the bodies had decomposed prior to their being placed there.

The great fortress of *Masada*, a national monument and source of inspiration to the State of Israel today, together with the mighty siege works of LEGIO X FRETENSIS, remain by the Dead Sea as a powerful reminder of both enormous courage and the dread military skill of Imperial Rome.

Military Equipment

Like the equipment of all armies before and since, the arms of Rome were subject to constant change, the major difference between modern war material and that of the ancient world being that almost all of the artefacts had to be made by hand prior to the Industrial Revolution which totally destroyed the individuality of armour and weapons.

For that reason, improvements in equipment took place relatively slowly, necessitating the continued use of material that was of considerable age, even if certain older items, helmets in particular, were relegated to inferior grades of soldier. It may be said with truth of Roman arms that as long as a piece remained in a serviceable condition, it continued to be used.

The longevity of certain types of material have caused some misconceptions to occur: a bronze helmet, for example, which may have been fashioned during the first century BC, could easily have remained in service throughout the first century AD, or even as late as the second century. Thus it is virtually impossible, or at least unwise, to attempt to date such objects by their find levels.

Body Armour

Other material, mail certainly, which was of a sturdy type of construction and unlikely to suffer damage to the extent that other forms of body defence obviously did, and for that reason has left fewer fragments to be discovered, gave rise to the belief that the Romans possessed only a small quantity of that material. This may be applied to many artefacts of iron, which, by its nature, is less likely to survive the intervening centuries than bronze, for example. This fact may be more clearly illustrated by the total absence to date of a specimen of a laminated arm defence (*manica*), either fragmentary or complete, although many sculptural and mosaic representations of such defences make it abundantly clear that they were quite common, for both gladiatorial and military use.

Misconceptions have also arisen as a result of incorrect interpretation of sculptural works. The great column in Rome, erected by the Emperor Marcus Ulpius Trajanus in the early years of the second century AD to commemorate his victories over the Dacians, portrays all the legionary infantry wearing laminated iron plate cuirasses (*loricae segmentatae*), whilst all the auxiliary forces are shown wearing defences of mail. Drawing upon

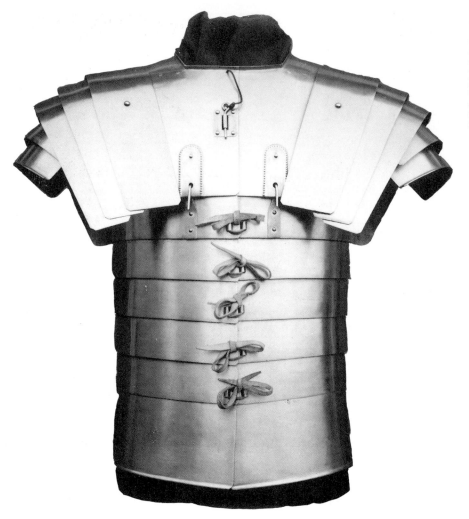

Laminated iron plate cuirass of Newstead type. This type of defence is to be seen on most of the representations of legionary infantry on Trajan's Column, Rome. Another version of this pattern probably had laminations carried up to the neck-opening. The Newstead type appeared during the second half of the first century AD. Author's reconstruction.

that immense sculptural work, many people in the field of history and costume in general have subscribed to the belief that iron plate armour of that type was confined to legionaries and that, consequently, where fragments of those cuirasses have been found, legionary infantry had been present.

However, it is now becoming clear that the armours in question were quite probably worn by the *auxilia* as well. A fragment of a triumphal monument found at Arlon, on the Belgium–Luxembourg border, portrays two cavalry troopers and part of a third, all clearly shown to wear body defences with shoulder-guards of laminated plate. The torsos, though, do not appear to be girt with segmented plate; a small slit at the lower edge of the foremost defence indicates that mail was intended by the sculptor. This is presumably a feature peculiar to cavalry riders, because the normal plate girdles of the *segmentata* would have rubbed against the pelvic bones and been most uncomfortable during a long period in the saddle. When worn

Part of a relief from a triumphal monument from Arlon, Belgium. The troopers wear helmets similar to the Weiler specimen (p. 147) and mail body defences with laminated plate shoulder-guards similar to those of the Corbridge *loricae segmentatae* (see p. 24).

by soldiers of the infantry *cohortes*, the normal *loricae* of Corbridge and Newstead patterns would not have presented any such difficulties; however, definite evidence of such armours being used in the auxiliary infantry has yet to be discovered.

The reliefs of Trajan's Column were probably executed in the manner described for two reasons. Firstly, the *lorica segmentata* is a much more aesthetically impressive defence and therefore visually dominant, which would enhance the appearance of the superior grade of troops; secondly, a clear distinction between the different classes of soldier was achieved by that means.

It is apparent that the artisans at the centre of the Empire were considerably less concerned over the accurate portrayal of individual types of equipment and though their products possess far greater artistic merit, their less well-schooled counterparts on the frontiers are much more reliable in that regard for our purposes, since they imitated, as far as the limitations of stone would permit, exactly what they saw every day of their lives.

Another area of misinterpretation has been caused by the common habit amongst ancient peoples of painting onto their sculptures fine details which were difficult to work with a chisel. This applies to various items, such as mail, military boots, groin-guard studs, baldric studs and fasteners, and perhaps even belt-plates in some instances.

This is, however, one area where Trajan's Column displays a greater degree of accuracy than many of the works from the frontiers, most particularly in the representation of mail, always a tedious business to portray in proper detail. The Romans simply worked the surface of the auxiliaries' defences with close-set vertical zigzag lines, which produced a very fair likeness of the texture required. An alternative method may be seen on the hauberk of the Celtic Warrior statue from Vachères and on several figures of legionaries on the Altar of Domitius Ahenobarbus in the Musée du Louvre: in those cases, the mail has been laboriously chiselled out with horizontal crescent cuts. Occasionally, a crude means of depicting mail may be encountered: the simple application of drill-holes.

Many other examples, which must obviously have been mail, but are now simply a smooth surface, were probably either just painted, or coated with gesso and the mail impressed into the surface with a curved tool before the plaster dried. The grave stele of *Centurio* Marcus Favonius Facilis in the Colchester and Essex Museum, Colchester, may have been finished out in the latter manner. As with so many products, costs may have been a governing consideration over the degree of excellence.

The origin of mail remains obscure. The earliest examples of that extraordinary material were found in Sarmatian and Scythian graves, dated to the fifth to sixth centuries BC, and one may conjecture that the invention of the material took place some considerable length of time before that period.

It has often been supposed that the Celts were the inventors of mail, a suggestion which is supported by an observation from the Roman historian Varro, who referred to Roman mail as 'Gallic'. Whilst there remains no means by which we may either prove or disprove Varro's statement, the Celts were certainly highly skilled metal-workers and so entirely capable of that innovation. One may, of course, say exactly the same of the Assyrians

---

PLATE 15   Two legionaries on guard duty at *Pergamon. c.* AD 200–250

The legionary on the left in this illustration is wearing a bronze helmet based on the skull-piece found at Niedermörmter near Xanten, Germany, in the collection of the Rheinisches Landesmuseum, Bonn. This piece is the last known helmet to be derived from the Gallic head-pieces of the first century BC; the multiple ribbing of the nape shows its ancestry. The cuirass is a possible development of the Newstead with a new form of latching device. The traditional *gladius* is giving way to a longer blade-form, more akin to a *spatha.* Scabbards now have large wheel-chapes and the baldric has become a very broad strap with elaborately pierced mounts. Whilst the men are shown to carry heavy *hastae* (thrusting spears), the *pilum* was apparently still carried by some units; indeed one grave stele shows a javelin with a double lead loading. One is inclined to feel that such a heavy weapon would have been extremely difficult to deliver. The shield is copied from the example excavated from the citadel of *Dura Europos* on the Euphrates river. This is the last shield which can be named *scutum* and is comparatively thin, so much so that many have thought it to be piece of parade equipment. The rim is bound with hide, instead of the expensive metal edging of earlier shields; perhaps the effects of economic pressures had begun to show.

The second legionary wears an iron helmet based on a badly preserved skull-piece from Hessen, Germany; much of this piece is the author's hypothesis. The cuirass has laminations which reach all the way up to the neck opening, a feature which is evidenced as early as the reign of Trajanus and is shown in several instances of later date. The wearing of *pteruges* is also quite commonly represented and certainly served to counter one of the *lorica segmentata*'s weaknesses: the vulnerability of the soldier's thighs. The *scutum* has been superseded by an almost circular flat shield; the horizontal hand-grip remains.

of the seventh to eighth century BC, who had been engaged in the manufacture of beautiful conical iron helmets, inlaid with bronze, long before
the technology required for the manufacture of such pieces had arrived in
Europe; or so we are led to believe by our current knowledge.

The Romans inherited two types of shoulder-doublings for their hauberks: one which had comparatively narrow shoulder 'straps', with ends
cut in a fashion reminiscent of similar parts of Greek linen cuirasses, and a
second pattern, more probably derived from earlier Celtic patterns, in the
form of a shoulder-cape, which required no backing leather, being simply
drawn about the wearer's shoulder girdle and secured with breast-hooks.

The latter pattern of doubling is indicated on numerous grave *stelae*
belonging to both standard-bearers and cavalrymen. The ordinary infantry
appear to have avoided using the cape type, favouring the Greek pattern,
perhaps in order to gain greater freedom of movement; the slight reduction
in weight is so little as to be insignificant. Future finds of *stelae* may alter
this belief. The Greek pattern required to be leathered, in order to keep the
mail spread to its proper shape. The leathering, whilst normally applied to
the rear of the mail, could be employed to provide a decorative facing to
the mail.

As a defensive material, mail has one major drawback: it was very
laborious to manufacture. The problem was partly overcome by the
introduction of alternate rows of punched rings, which did not require to
be joined; thus reducing the overall time in manufacture by as much as a
quarter. The punched rings still had to be linked together with riveted wire
ones, or could be left as a simple butted circlet, without riveting. The latter
was, of course, not as strong as riveted work, but the cost would again have
been greatly reduced.

The production of the riveted rings, judging by surviving examples,
appears to have been identical to the method used in later ages. First, the

PLATE 16   A *decurio* and trooper of a cavalry *ala* inside a milecastle on Hadrian's Wall. First half
of the third century AD

The helmets of these two cavalrymen are based on a most beautiful example of Auxiliary Cavalry type 'H', found at Heddernheim, Germany, in the collection of the Frankfurt Museum. These magnificently decorated head-pieces are a clear indication of the rise of the importance of the cavalry as an independent strikng field force. The *antha* on the crown of the original helmet is pierced with a circular hole, thought to have held a hair streamer as shown. Arming doublets with *pteruges* are worn by both men, but only a single-layer kilt for the trooper. The corselet is a new scale construction which required no foundation; each scale was linked not only to its horizontal neighbours, but vertically as well. The fact that this rendered the corselet fairly inflexible meant that it could only cover the same area of the torso as a short muscled cuirass. The scabbards of the *spathae* now have wheel-chapes and decorative bronze loops pinned to the upper end for the baldric. The shields are almost circular and have hide-bound rims.

A thousand-strong unit of these men, such as the ALA PETRIANA, must have presented a considerable deterrent to any would-be attacker from the north of the Wall. They were housed in forts with three double gates to the north, so that a rapid sortie could be mounted and the enemy cut off from his means of escape.

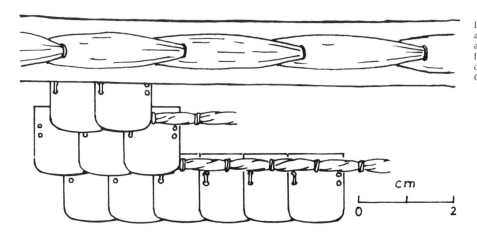

Detail of restored bronze scale armour, showing its construction and neck-leathering. The original fragment of a corselet was found in a ditch of the Severan fortress at Carpow, Scotland.

wire had to be drawn to the desired gauge; this was most important, since the weight of the finished hauberk would be greatly increased if a wire of too large a diameter was used. Whilst there has been some doubt as to the Romans' ability to produce wire in such a fashion, it was probably made by steadily reducing a rod by drawing it through progressively smaller holes in a thick plate; the initial rod would have been made by hammerwork.

The next step was to coil the wire round a core and chisel along the resulting spring form, producing circlets with offset ends. These were then forced through a tapering hole in a block, which caused the ends to overlap. In that form, the individual rings were placed in a special pair of tongs and their ends flattened, ready for piercing with a second pair of tongs with a claw in the jaws. The rings were then ready for insertion into the piece of mail. The 'rivet' used to secure the rings was simply a small triangular chip of metal, closed with a third pair of tongs with recessed jaws.

The weight of Roman hauberks varied considerably, the heaviest being some 7 kg (16 lb), which compares most favourably with more recent mail defences; some Sudanese examples, from the second half of the nineteenth century, weigh as much as 13.5 kg (30 lb). In order to prevent the entire weight of the mail falling on the wearer's shoulders, the Romans used the beautifully metalled military belt, which distributed part of the load onto the hips, as well as providing carriage for sidearms. Shorter hauberks, which were much lighter, were often worn unbelted.

Extremely fine Roman mail, thought logically to be that of the officer class, was made from rings which could measure as little as 4 mm ($^5/_{32}$ in) outside diameter, often, if not always, of bronze. Some of the fine mail was faced with tiny scales, each scale being attached to the hauberk by passing four of the rings through a right-angled ledge at the top of each scale. Though such defences would appear to have been immensely costly, the number of fragments of individual shirts seems to convey that they were quite common.

Defences of scale, being the earliest known armour made from metal,

128

were always present in the Roman army, in a great variety of sizes and designs of scale. Though mail was a superior form of defence, scale, because no great degree of skill in manufacture was needed, was cheaper to produce and provided a more readily available armour for the lower grades of soldier, in its simpler forms.

The structure of the majority of those defences is clearly shown by a rare find from the 1979 excavations of the Severan fortress at Carpow, Perthshire, Scotland. The bronze scales of the Carpow find, being quite small and thin, probably those of a shirt belonging to a junior officer, have not survived the centuries in a good state of preservation and are in a very fragmentary condition. Despite the poor condition of the scales, the coarse linen foundation of two-over-one twill is well preserved, as are the stitching threads of linen yarn. The scales were linked together in horizontal rows, with each scale overlapping its neighbour, fastened together with loose wire rings passed through the side holes. The linked rows were then placed on the foundation, starting at the lower edge of the defence and stitched down by placing a strand of yarn along the upper line of holes, with the attaching thread being passed over the yarn.

Since the Carpow fragment is the only piece of scale armour to retain its foundation and stitching threads intact, it is not possible to state categorically that this was the only method of stitching ever used; however, it seems to be the most satisfactory way of minimising the likelihood of damage by fraying in normal wear. Less fine defences sometimes had straw inserted behind the scales to help reduce damage to the foundation, a practice which would obviously have interfered with the function of the Carpow structure.

The defensive quality of scale was only fair. The scales of infantry hauberks were never thick enough to withstand a sound blow and remain undamaged. Perhaps a more serious deficiency lies in the fact that such defences could be quite readily pierced by an upthrust of sword or spear; a hazardous aspect of which many cavalry riders must have been acutely aware, when engaging foot-soldiers armed with pole weapons.

This weakness was overcome, certainly by the third century AD, as far as the cavalry were concerned, when a new form of scale linkage was introduced. The scales, of relatively large dimensions, were linked together with wire rings both horizontally and vertically, which rendered the use of a foundation unnecessary. Whilst this innovation improved such defences in one way, it detracted from their usefulness in another, by making the armour virtually inflexible, so that it could only be employed on areas of the body where little or no movement was required, that is the same coverage as that afforded by the short plate cuirasses of a horse man's pattern, which reach only to the lower extremity of the rib-cage and do not cover the deltoids of the wearer.

That innovation did not preclude the continued manufacture of scale armour of the earlier construction, indeed the latter was extended to include horse-bards for the *cataphractarii* of the third century. Two examples of bards were discovered at the frontier bastion of *Dura Europos* on the river Euphrates: one with bronze scales, now in the National Museum, Damascus; the other of iron, now in the John Woodman Higgins Armory Museum, Worcester, Massachusetts. As they stand, the bards provide only partial protection for the animals they were designed to guard against injury and it is logical to assume that there were originally other parts attached to them, specifically for the defence of the breast, neck and head.

A relief from the Arch of Constantine in Rome, dating from the early fourth century, depicts the cavalry of Constantinus defeating that of his rival Maxentius at the battle of Pons Milvius. Whilst the mounts of the Maxentian troopers are not in view, their riders are, wearing long scale defences, with mid-arm-length sleeves. Those men are considered to have been *cataphractarii* and their mounts would most probably have been equipped with bards of the Dura type.

Horse armour of that kind may, in fact, have appeared in the Roman army somewhat earlier than our knowledge, based upon sculptural evidence, suggests. The Romans had certainly encountered adversaries armoured in that fashion as early as the Trajanic wars against the Dacians; for Sarmatian cataphracts are depicted on Trajan's Column, though rather fancifully, being pursued by Roman cavalry. Thus one may expect that evidence of those heavily armoured horsemen in the Roman forces as early as the second century AD may one day be discovered.

Helmets

The majority of the bronze Roman infantry helmets that survive from the first century BC are of relatively poor quality in their finish, when compared to those of the preceding century. The reason for that decline in workmanship may be found to have originated in the latter part of the Jugurthine War under Marius. Contrary to custom, Marius, in order to

---

PLATE 17   Cavalry in an eastern province engage in the *hippika gymnasia*. Mid-third century AD

This illustration clearly shows the high degree of embellishment that had been achieved in sports equipment by this date, though the helmets lack much of the artistic merit of those of the first century AD. The body defences of scale are constructed in the same manner as the inflexible field corselets of the time, but are known to have been fitted with small breast-plates, which opened to admit the wearer's head. The introduction of *pteruges* probably occurred during the late second century AD; these would most probably have been made from linen for this purpose. The most remarkable aspect of the third-century equipment is the greaves. They are decorated in very high relief and have separate knee-guard parts hinged to the shin section. A large hoard of third-century sports equipment was discovered at Straubing in Bavaria, now in the Straubing Museum, consisting of several greaves, helmets and chamfrons for the ponies. The metals shown in the plate are largely drawn from the Straubing find.

The rider carrying the standard is a *draconarius*, named after the *draco* or dragon standard which may be seen being carried with Sarmatian cataphracts on Trajan's Column. After the annexation of Dacia, the *draco* was adopted into the Roman army.

secure sufficient enlistment for his campaigns, had thrown service with the legions open to the landless poor. In consequence of that action, a great many of the recruits did not possess the means to purchase expensive equipment for themselves, which must therefore have been provided by the State, even if deductions were later made from the soldiers' pay to defray the cost. Issue pieces of the kind were bound to be less ornate than their counterparts ordered by wealthy individuals, a number of which survive and display a very high measure of skill in their metalwork.

To date, no example of the cheek-guards that belonged to the issue class of helmet, called today Montefortino type 'C', has been identified; probably because many such head-pieces ended their days as bronze buckets, with their cheek-guards removed for that purpose. The type shown on the author's reconstruction is hypothetical, being based on an earlier example in the Museo Stibbert, Florence.

The cresting of the Montefortino helments was usually of horse-hair, secured with a simple pin inserted into the lead-filled knob on the helmet's crown: an odd arrangement which left the crest free to revolve and could leave the hair tail in front of the wearer's face; furthermore, it was extremely easy to dislodge from its mounting, unless there was originally

Bronze legionary helmet of Montefortino type 'C', based on a skull-piece said to have been found in Iran. The cheek-guards are hypothetical. Helmets of this type were mass-produced during the early years of the first century BC. Author's reconstruction.

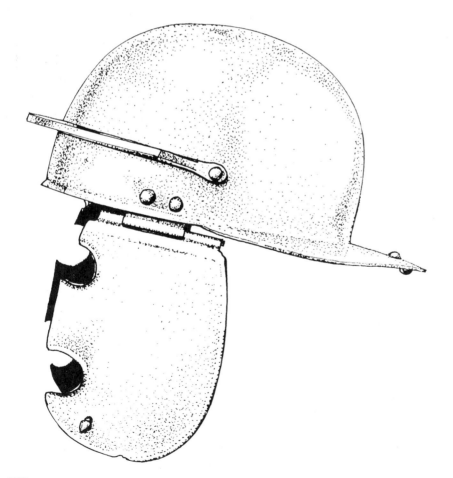

Bronze infantry helmet of Coolus type 'C', from Schaan, Liechtenstein. One of two almost identical helmets, neither of which was ever fitted with cresting. Head-pieces of this type date from the late first century BC. In the collection of the Schweizerisches Landesmuseum, Zürich.

Iron legionary infantry helmet of Imperial Gallic type 'F', with a horse-hair crest of Celtic type. Second quarter of the first century AD.

a thong on the crest box, which could be tied round the base of the crest-knob. These facts are somewhat surprising, since crests were worn in action at the time, a matter clearly attested by Gaius Julius Caesar in his *Commentaries* on the Gallic War.

A more anatomical form of skull-piece probably began to supersede the Montefortino pattern during the second half of the first century BC. The new pattern, called 'Coolus' after a find made near the village of Coole in the Marne basin, was in process of development by the Gallic Celts as early as the fourth century BC, reaching its purest form by the end of the second century BC, being devoid of almost all decoration and extraneous fittings, except for cheek-guards. Whilst the earliest examples of such helmets, known to have been in service with the Roman army, are very similar in respect of decoration and have no fittings for the mounting of a crest, the Romans introduced a heavy frontal reinforce or peak, which prevented blows from striking that area, which was comparatively weak. The concept of strengthening the front of a helmet skull by introducing an angle may be seen in earlier Greek helmets. A rare find from Oberaden in Germany, of an iron Coolus skull of the late first century BC–early first century AD pattern, though unfortunately destroyed in World War II, proves that such head-pieces were also made in that metal, though in what relative quantity remains unknown.

The addition of a crest-knob followed, with a slot cut into the top to take a comparative fitting, presumably in the underside of the crest-box. The whole was then secured by means of a pin passed through both box and knob from the side, eliminating any movement. The appearance of the crest itself was slightly different to those of the Montefortino helmets, in that it had a short forward brush as well as a long tail of hair. There were probably also transverse versions with equal lengths of hair for centurial use (see author's reconstruction p. 134).

Conquest of other nations whose metallurgical technology was in advance of that of the factories of Italy produced profound changes in Roman equipment. Caesar's subjugation of Gaul in the mid-first century BC, in particular, brought not only the makers of the simpler forms of Gallic head-piece within the Roman sphere, but also the armourers whose knowledge of iron-working appears to have been drawn upon for the more complex styles of legionary infantry helmet, known today as of Imperial Gallic type.

The earliest Roman iron helmet of that class (Imperial Gallic type 'A') was found at Nijmegen. The identifying features of nape and neck-guard ribbing, eyebrows and cheek-guard panelling, which clearly define the Gallic origins of the piece, continue in helmets of that classification, in one way or another, until the third century, when Gallic influence appears to have ceased and patterns of Sassanid Persian construction became the norm.

Bronze helmets of Coolus type continued to be made concurrently with the Imperial Gallic pattern, increasing in the size of the neck-guard until

133

the second quarter of the first century AD, when the two surviving specimens of the largest type were probably made (Coolus type 'G'). Both of those helmets, one from Drusenheim, near Hagenau, the second from the river Danube near Burlafingen in Bavaria, have flat, almost semi-circular neck-guards and tall bulbous skulls of nearly circular plan. The cheek-guards are missing from both specimens; the type shown in the illustration of the reconstructed Hagenau helmet is based on an example from the Rhine at Mainz, now in the Museum of Antiquities, Newcastle upon Tyne, England.

A legionary iron helmet recovered from the river Kupa in Yugoslavia represents Imperial Gallic type 'C'. The absence of ear-guards, the neck-guard piping being carried round the ear recesses, indicates that the piece was made in either the late first century BC, or the early first century AD. The original helmet lacks its peak, brow-band and crest tie fittings; but is otherwise reasonably well-preserved.

The author's reconstruction (p. 133) of a legionary iron helmet of type 'F' shows a complete example based on a skull fragment in the collection of the Römisch-Germanisches Zentralmuseum, Mainz, which consists of an

Bronze helmet of Coolus type 'E'. Author's reconstruction, crested in the early style of a centurion. Late first century BC to early first century AD.

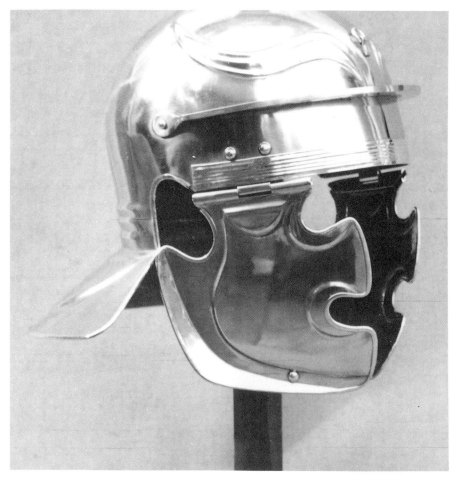

Iron legionary infantry helmet of Imperial Gallic type 'C', based on the specimen recovered from the river Kupa in Yugoslavia. The absence of ear-guards indicates manufacture in the late first century BC to early first century AD. The original helmet is in the collection of the Archaeological Museum, Zagreb. Author's reconstruction.

almost complete bowl, lacking its nape and neck-guard, and the cheek-guards. The latter parts are based on those of a contemporary skull from Sisak, Yugoslavia, and a cheek-guard from Hod Hill, Dorset, England. The cheek-guards of the reconstruction have been given the maximum number of decorative bosses usually employed, in order to match those of the Mainz skull; the original Hod Hill cheek-guard had only one, or possibly a silvered rivet. Evidence shows that often some, if not all, of the bronze piping and fittings of such helmets were tinned or silvered, which seems a curious practice, since the difference in the colours of the bronze and the iron greatly enhances the beauty of these head-pieces, at least in modern eyes. Perhaps the Roman associated bronze with a poorer class of equipment and therefore the more silvery he looked, the wealthier and more god-like he felt himself to be.

The cresting shown is of a Celtic type, presumed to have been used in conjunction with the known crest-stands and other fastenings associated with head-pieces of Imperial Gallic and Italic type. Common though such cresting obviously was, it is, to date, unknown in Roman sculpture. The only clear representation of such a form of crest is to be found on the figure of a Celtic horseman embossed on the Gundestrup cauldron from Jutland, now in the Nationalmuseet, Copenhagen.

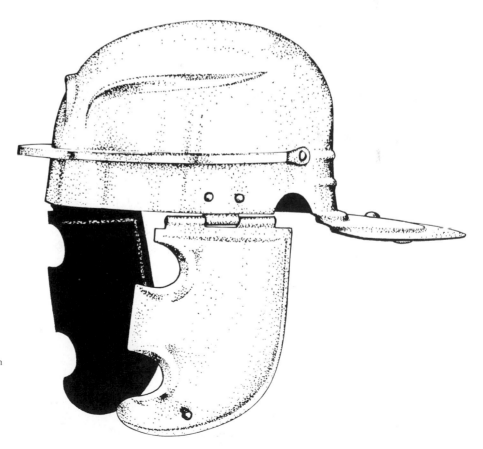

Iron infantry helmet of Imperial Gallic type 'A', from a reconstruction by the late H.R. Robinson, based on the specimen found near the fort at Nijmegen, Netherlands. Probably made in the late Augustan period. The original helmet is in the collection of the Rijksmuseum G.M. Kam, Nijmegen.

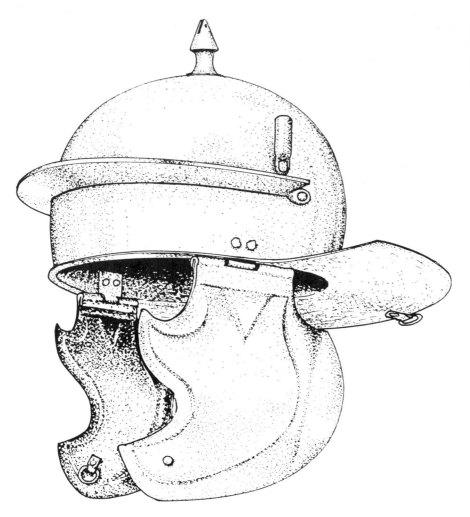

Bronze infantry helmet of Coolus type 'G'. From a reconstruction by the late H.R. Robinson. The skull-piece was found at Drusenheim near Hagenau; the cheek-guards are based on a specimen from the river Rhine at Mainz. The skull is in the collection of the Hagenau Museum.

Helmets of Italian manufacture, which may be of similar date to Imperial Gallic 'F', are difficult to determine. The helmet denoted Imperial Italic type 'C', which is one of two very similar head-pieces recovered from the river Po near Cremona, was most probably lost during the civil war of AD 68–69. However, precisely when the pieces were actually made is uncertain and the pattern may be as early as the second quarter of that century. Alternatively, the extremely rough workmanship displayed by both helmets may indicate that they were made during the time of emergency occasioned by the onset of the civil war.

The more elaborate iron helmet of Imperial Italic type 'D' with applied bronze ornament, recovered from the river Rhine at Mainz, may also date from the second quarter of the first century AD. Whilst both of the helmets 'C' and 'D' show attempts to copy some of the features of Imperial Gallic helmets, notably the nape ribs and neck-guard steps, the demonic eyebrows have been avoided. The reason for that omission may lie in the fact that the embossing of eyebrows is a highly-skilled operation, which had

Bronze helmet of Imperial Italic type 'C', recovered from the river Po near Cremona. Thought to have been lost during the civil war of AD 68–69. In the collection of the Museo Stibbert, Florence.

Iron legionary infantry helmet of Imperial Gallic type 'J', based on the remains of a helmet from the fort of *Brigetio*, Hungary. Probably Italian manufacture of the late first century AD.

been employed by the Gallic armourers, certainly from the mid-first century BC onward, but proved to be rather too advanced for the artisans of Italy at that period of time.

Helmets of Gallic pattern were also produced in bronze and were probably common. An almost complete specimen of such a helmet was found at *Aquincum*, near Budapest, Hungary, now in the Aquincum Museum. This helmet, similar in many respects to a skull-piece recovered from the river Rhine at Mainz, now in the Germanisches Nationalmuseum, Nuremberg, Germany, though denoted Imperial Gallic type 'I', was probably of Italian manufacture. The cheek-guard pattern and method of panelling are of Italic type, as is the heavy crest-stand soldered to the crown; the latter was probably also attached to the Mainz specimen, where now only a circular patch of solder remains. The origin of these two helmets may be thus: the Mainz skull-piece certainly belonged to LEGIO I ADIUTRIX and would appear to have been lost to the Rhine before AD 83, when a bridge was built at Mainz, which made the river-crossing safe. The Aquincum helmet may have belonged to LEGIO II ADIUTRIX, which arrived at *Aquincum* about AD 106. Since both of those legions were being raised by the Emperor Nero in AD 68 for a campaign in the Caucasus when the civil war began and were finally brought into service by Vespasian, though LEGIO I ADIUTRIX saw some action during that conflict, it is just possible that both pieces were made after the war was over and were made from bronze because of the necessity of replacing losses incurred during the disturbance.

Another Imperial Gallic helmet which may have been an Italian manufacture was found on the site of the fort of *Brigetio*, on the Danube

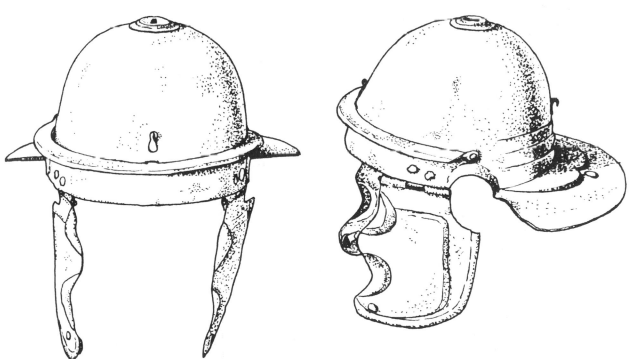

frontier. That 'J' type helmet bears several close similarities to the Aquincum helmet, particularly in respect of the basic shape of the skull and neck-guard, and the form of the cheek-guards. Also like the 'I' type helmets, the Brigetio helmet has a circular mark on the top of the skull, which could readily have been the position of a crest stand similar in

Iron infantry helmet of Imperial Italic type 'D'. This helmet, elaborately decorated with thin bronze sheet, was recovered from the river Rhine at Mainz. Probably made in the late second quarter of the first century AD. In the collection of the Worms Museum.

PLATE 18   A force of Roman infantry has been defeated by Sassanian Persian cavalry. A standard-bearer attempts to escape, aided by a Roman cataphract. Mesopotamia, third century AD

The *cataphractarius* engaging the Persian is largely based on paintings discovered at *Dura Europos* on the river Euphrates, where two bards coated with scale armour for horses were also found, though lacking the parts for the protection of the animals' heads. The hood of the rider is most unusual and is unknown from any other source.

The standard-bearer is based on the grave *stela* of a *signifer* found at the fort at Carrawburgh on Hadrian's Wall, now in the collection of the Clayton Museum, Chesters Fort, Hadrian's Wall. All body armour has been discarded by the infantry, who now rely on large shields for protection; but this standard-bearer is shown to have an oddly shaped and relatively small shield, though no smaller than the *parmae* carried by the earlier men of his rank. The *signum* portrayed on the stele is a *Taurus*; but precisely what size of unit came under these small insignia is obscure. Others of this type have been found and seem to be normally Zodiac signs, excluding the example from *Vindolanda* near Hadrian's Wall, which is a horse, possibly a wingless Pegasus.

appearance to that of the Aquincum piece. The author's reconstruction (p. 137) is fitted with the alternative Italian crest attachment, a flat, slotted stand-holder, which held a stand similar to those of Imperial Gallic type. Whether the Brigetio helmet's crest was tied to rings, or to hooks as shown, is not certain; however, in the light of the Aquincum find, rings would now appear more likely.

By the end of the first century AD, or early in the second, the Italian armourers had evolved a class of iron head-piece with crossed skull reinforces of half-round section running over the crown. Helmets of this type are clearly represented on the metopes of the *Tropaeum Trajani* at Adamklissi near the Black Sea in Romania, dating from the early second century. The most complete example of such a helmet (Imperial Italic type 'G'), was said to have been found in a cave at Hebron, Israel. The piece was of a strong construction, with quite simple decoration in the form of applied thin bronze sheet and with shallow panelling to the cheek-guards and comparative nape and neck-guard ribs.

Iron infantry helmet of Romano-Sassanian type, based on a specimen found at *Augusta Raurica* (Augst), Switzerland. Late third to fourth century AD.

The legionary infantry helmet of the second to third centuries developed a much deeper nape, similar to the cavalry helmets of the late first to mid-second century, and in the case of the Imperial Italic type 'H' specimen from Niedermörmter near Xanten, a massive neck-guard; the dimensions of which feature were probably governed by the nature of the metal, for an iron skull-piece of similar date and depth of nape, found at Hessen, now in the Frankfurt Museum, has a comparatively small neck-guard. The same difference may be observed between the deep cavalry helmets of iron and bronze.

The Niedermörmter skull is the last known Roman helmet to display Gallic origins, by the ribbing of the nape and a strip of pearled decoration, notched at the centre to represent the neck-guard steps.

With the expansion in the Middle East of Sassanian Persia, which had overtaken Rome's old enemy the Parthians, serious conflict developed in that region, which brought the Romans into contact with a new method of helmet manufacture. The principle of making the new fabricated skull-pieces meant an enormous, and doubtless very welcome, saving in the manufacturing time and skill required.

The Roman infantry helmets basically consisted of two halves, riveted together with a central comb. The cheek-guards were rather poor; whilst they covered the wearer's ears, they left much of the face exposed. The neck-guard on the other hand, being suspended from leathers, remained in contact with the nape of the neck, regardless of what angle was adopted by the wearer's head.

The edges of the skull and associated plates appear to have been piped, presumably with hide, stitched to the helmets through multiple holes close to the extremities of the plates. The decorative effect of the piping was sometimes copied in applied bronze ribbon; evidenced by a fourth-century neck-guard of relatively angular form, from the fort at Richborough, Kent. Whether that piece belonged to an infantry or cavalry head-piece is not

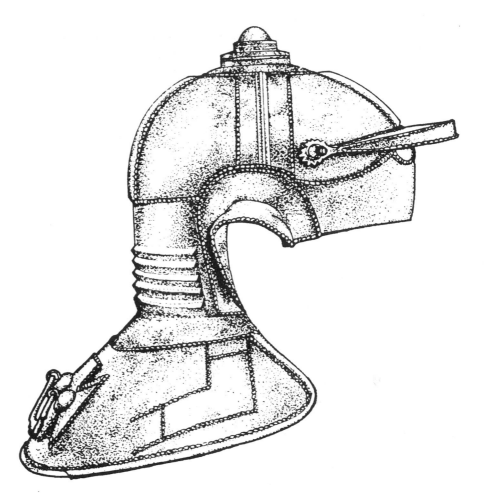

Bronze infantry helmet of Imperial Italic type 'H' found at Niedermörmter, near Xanten. This piece is the last known example of a Roman infantry helmet descended from the Gallic pattern. Probably made in the late second or early third century AD. In the collection of the Rheinisches Landesmuseum, Bonn.

possible to determine with absolute certainty; however, the method of suspension suggests the infantry.

With the enlistment of auxiliary troops into the Roman army on a permanent basis during the reign of Augustus, it appears that it was necessary for soldiers who were not already equipped with the arms of their native countries to be supplied with armour and weapons by the Roman State upon acceptance for service.

Whilst many Montefortino and Coolus helmets doubtless found their way into the *auxilia,* the first helmets which can be definitely identified as being of auxiliary type are thought to have originated in the mid-first century AD. The two helmets in question were both made by metal 'spinning', a production process still widely used today in the manufacture of many circular metal objects, which is carried out by forcing a disc of metal, in Roman work annealed bronze, over a former of either wood or metal, revolving in a type of lathe. The Roman machines were most probably powered by water-wheels, in much the same way as their larger grain mills were operated; a late example of such a mill may be seen today at Barbegal in southern France. One may surmise that all the machinery of

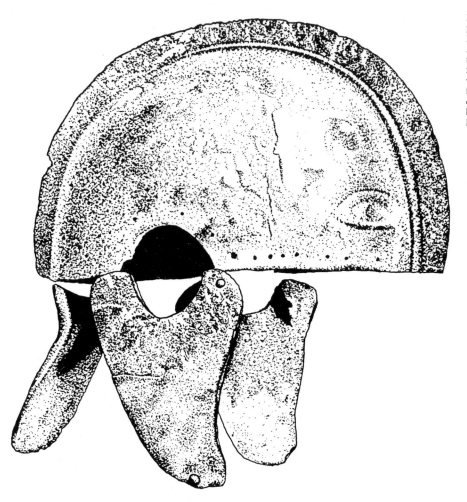

Iron infantry helmet with a skull-piece fabricated in two halves. Found with three similar helmets at *Intercisa*, Hungary. Simple helmets of this pattern were developed from Sassanian Persian head-pieces and were common in the late third to fourth century AD. The neck and cheek-guards were suspended by leathers. In the collection of the National Museum, Budapest.

PLATE 19   Gothic warriors surprise a Roman infantry unit near the river Danube. Late third century AD

The Roman infantry are now devoid of body armour as increasing barbarian influence enters the army; the *gladius* too has long since disappeared. The soldiers now have only their huge circular shields and Romano-Sassanian helmets as defences. Very few of the ordinary infantry head-pieces are known to have survived from this period; however, those that exist are all basically of the same pattern: two halves, riveted together with a central comb. Sometimes these helmets were crested, presumably with a horse-hair brush, or with feathers. One of the four specimens recovered from *Intercisa* in Hungary, now in the Hungarian National Museum, Budapest, is fitted with an iron plate crest. In all cases the cheek-guards and neck-guards were suspended from the skull-pieces with leathers and apparently piped with hide as shown. They were certainly very much easier to make than the earlier helmets with single-piece skulls, no doubt a relief when many of the men capable of making them may have perished in the serious plague during the reign of Gallus in the middle years of the third century.

Items upon which a good deal of time seems to have been quite needlessly expended, when it could have been better employed, are the belt fittings. Many of these are painstakingly chip-carved bronze, most skilfully made, but serving little purpose other than to cause the warrior to feel less poorly armed. The men also now wear what may have still been called *bracae*, the rather scathing Roman term for the trousers of barbarians, expressed in the term *bracati*.

the larger Roman arms workshops were powered by that means, as they were in medieval times; indeed, such a power-source was still in use for the manufacture of agricultural implements up to the early Industrial Revolution. Precisely when the spinning process was invented is not known, but it may well pre-date the reign of Augustus.

The first of the helmets denoted Auxiliary Infantry type 'A' was found at Alem, in Noord-Brabant, Netherlands, now in the private collection of Dr S.M. van Ommeren, Elst (Utr.). The piece represents an extraordinarily poor example of helmet-making and was produced by spinning down a long tubular shape, closed at one end with a dome. The spinning was then cut to remove the face area beneath the brow and the remaining part worked upwards to form the neck-guard, with the result that the outer edge was always extremely thin. Since that helmet was obviously never intended for legionary use, and carries the punched names of two centurions, attesting to that fact, it seems strange that the helmet, crude as it is, carries mountings for a central crest and side-plumes. The only logical explanation for this is the possibility that the owner, though serving in the *auxilia*, was a Roman citizen, perhaps the son of a time-expired auxiliary, who joined his father's old unit when he came of age. At least, a more plausible explanation is yet to be found.

A heavier and better-made spun skull-piece of Auxiliary Infantry type 'A' is shown in the author's reconstruction of the specimen from Flüren in Germany, now in the Rheinisches Landesmuseum, Bonn. Instead of working the disc of metal all the way down, as with the Alem piece, the

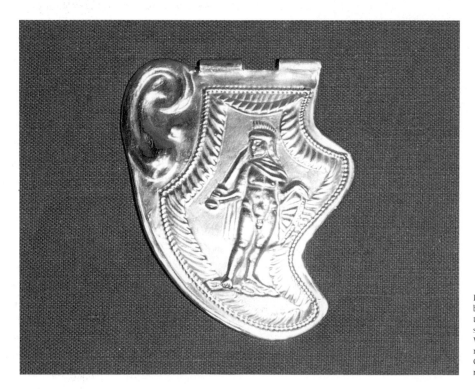

Iron cheek-guard with embossed bronze skinning of Auxiliary Cavalry type 'A', author's copy of the specimen recovered from the river Waal, near Yrendoorn, Netherlands, now in the Rijksmuseum van Oudheden, Leiden. Probably mid-first century AD.

Roman spinner left a thick flange at the base of the skull form, which was then cut away to leave the neck-guard at almost the finished angle. The cheek-guards used in the reconstruction are copied from an example found at Büderich, which is in the same collection.

Auxiliary infantry helmets were also made from beaten plate. A complete example of one of those of type 'B' was recovered from the river Rhine at Mainz, now in the Mittelrheinisches Landesmuseum, Mainz. The simple bronze head-piece is of a sturdy and sensible design, similar in some respects to the legionary helmets of the same period. In common with the Flüren skull, no provisions were ever made for cresting.

The early auxiliary cavalry appear to have been equipped with Coolus helmets and possibly others of simple Gallic form; or so they are portrayed on the battle reliefs of the Arch of Orange in France, which was erected to commemorate the suppression by LEGIO II AUGUSTA of a Gallic revolt in AD 22.

The first true Roman cavalry helmets, Auxiliary Cavalry type 'A', are

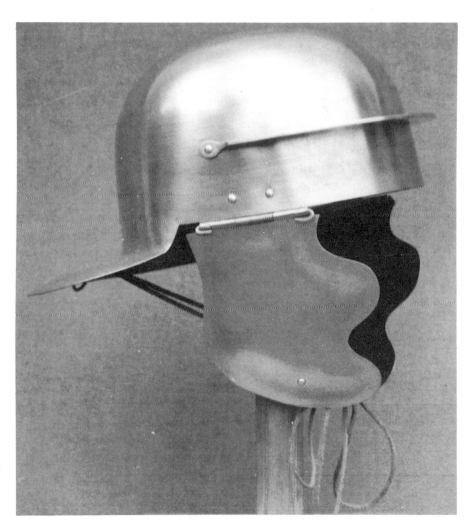

Bronze helmet of Auxiliary Infantry type 'A', based on the spun skull-piece from Flüren and a cheek-guard from Büderich, Germany. The piece was probably made during the mid-first century AD. Author's reconstruction.

145

Bronze helmet of Auxiliary Infantry type 'B'. Recovered from the river Rhine at Mainz, the head-piece was probably made during the second half of the first century AD. In the collection of the Mittelrheinisches Landesmuseum, Mainz.

represented by an almost complete example recovered from a cremation grave near to the small village of Weiler, in Luxembourg. Helmets of that type were probably made during either the fourth quarter of the first century BC, or the first quarter of the first century AD. The skull of the Weiler helmet, now completely oxidised, was a heavy iron piece, some 3 mm (⅛ in) in thickness, embossed with concentric rows of small curlets, given greater definition by ball-punching from the inside of the skull. The brow edge was fitted with a finely decorated applied bronze strip, similar to the iron legionary infantry helmets. The surviving cheek-guard is the earliest known example of thin bronze skinning over iron plate, though the finish was absolutely plain except for a slightly raised rib at the edge. The absence of ear-guards is an indication of the piece's early date and the pattern's continued use is next evidenced by a fragment of the skull of an apparently identical helmet, which was found on the site of the fort at Longthorpe, near Peterborough, which was probably built shortly after an abortive uprising by the Iceni in AD 48. A clear sculptural representation of the Weiler pattern is to be found on the grave *stela* of the cavalry trooper Titus Flavius Bassus, who served with the ALA NORICUM in the mid-second

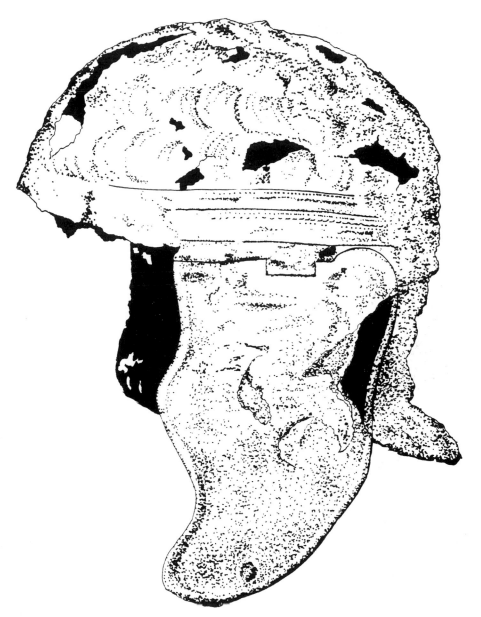

Iron helmet of Auxiliary Cavalry type 'A', found in a grave near the village of Weiler in Luxembourg. The helmet has an applied bronze brow band and bronze skinning to the iron cheek-guards. Probable date of manufacture early first century AD.

half of the first century AD, in the collection of the Römisch-Germanisches Museum, Cologne.

The life-span of a head-piece of such a thickness must have been considerable and they clearly existed concurrently with a later pattern represented by a skull-piece found on the site of the fort at Northwich, Cheshire, England. The author's reconstruction, now on display at the Salt Museum, Northwich, shows the skull coupled with a pattern of cheek-guard based on the remains of a bronze skinning of suitable type, which was found at Stanwix, Carlisle; now in the Tullie House Museum, Carlisle. The Northwich skull was thinner than Weiler, being 2 mm (5/64 in) thick, but remains a good strong field helmet. The style of the hair, which was simply chased in from the outside with considerable force, is markedly different to Weiler. This pattern is again clearly represented in sculpture on the Rhine frontier and may be seen on the grave stele of the trooper Gaius Romanius, who also served with the ALA NORICUM at about the same time as Bassus (Mittelrheinisches Landesmuseum, Mainz). The Northwich pattern, however, has ear-guards, with a fine reeded edge to the flange; the addition of those fittings, occasioned by the narrowing of the skull-piece as against the almost circular Weiler type, suggests that the Northwich helmet was of a slightly later date. The oddly high-angled brow edge of Northwich is probably a feature peculiar to a certain workshop and not indicative of its date in relation to other specimens.

The practice of fitting iron cavalry helmets with complete skinning of either bronze or silver appears to have commenced in the middle years of the first century AD. The specimen found at Witcham Gravel, Cambridge-shire, England, of Auxiliary Cavalry type 'B', now in the British Museum, has a slightly larger neck-guard than its predecessors, ornamented with huge bosses, six in number in its complete state, and small bosses, probably of plain type, five to each cheek-guard. Marks on the pate-skin show that there was originally a crest-box which was attached directly to the skull: the only surviving helmet which gives evidence of the existence of such a crest, so often depicted in sculptural works. A circular patch of solder on the front of the brow-plate was probably the position occupied by a Medusa mask.

Another example of a skinned cavalry helmet, now in the Mittelrhein-isches Museum, Koblenz, has a pate-skin beautifully embossed with fine hair curlets. Unfortunately, apart from the upper portion of the iron skull and one ear-guard, nothing more remains of that important piece. However,

Iron helmet of Auxiliary Cavalry type 'E'. Late first century AD to mid-second century.

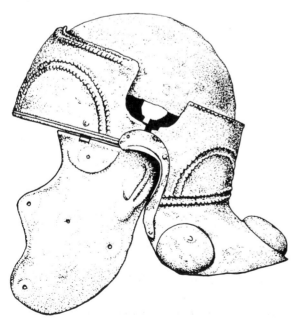

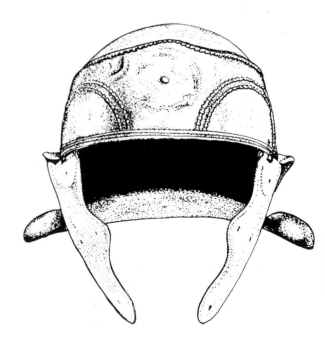

Chased iron helmet of Auxiliary Cavalry type 'A', based on a skull-piece from the fort at Northwich, Cheshire, and the remains of a cheek-guard skinning from Stanwix, near Carlisle on Hadrian's Wall.

Opposite:
Iron cavalry helmet with applied bronze skinning of Auxiliary Cavalry type 'B', from Witcham Gravel, Cambridgeshire. Probably made in the second quarter of the first century AD. In the collection of the British Museum.

marks on the surviving elements show that it was originally fitted with a peak, presumably of thin sheet metal. That new feature probably dates the helmet's manufacture to the third to fourth quarter of the first century AD; the peak became a regular addition to cavalry helmets thereafter.

The first evidence for the introduction of the fearsome iron cavalry helmets of type 'E', with crossed skull reinforces secured with conical rivets (see author's reconstruction opposite), occurs on the grave *stela* of the trooper Dolanus, now in the Städtisches Museum, Wiesbaden, dated to the late first century AD. The deeper nape afforded far more protection to the trooper's neck against a back-hand sword cut, and the flanged cheek-guards, which in one case almost sat on the wearer's thorax, gave better defence to the throat than earlier patterns. The latched overlap at the jaw is a feature which began with these helmets and continued up to the end of the second century.

Whilst there is as yet no sculptural evidence to support the fact, the presence of plume-tubes on one example prove that at least some of the 'E' type cavalry helmets were crested; perhaps here again, it was a matter of the citizen status of the wearer, or indeed of the entire unit. None of the surviving iron specimens is fitted with any kind of special attachments for the mounting of a central crest; and presumably the ends of the box were tied to the rivets at terminations of the longitudinal reinforce. This could also have applied to the lower-grade bronze counterparts of these helmets, which used ball-headed rivets instead of conical ones.

The bronze versions that survive were of an inferior standard of finish generally, without any piping to the cheek-guards or applied ornamental plating. They were provided with the same jaw overlap and sometimes an external strap from the rear of the cheek-guards, which buckled behind the nape of the skull. Helmets of that type, denoted Auxiliary Cavalry 'F', because of their plainer design, are considered to be those which belonged to *cohortes equitatae*.

During the late second century, a far more elaborately decorated class of cavalry helmet appeared. The example illustrated (p. 154) was found at Heddernheim and is now in the Frankfurt Museum. The helmet was of iron basically, with applied bronze sheet, engraved and embossed with designs of Thracian origin. As was the case with all other helmets of that class, the Heddernheim specimen was fitted with a peak, which was seated along the top of the brow-plate, secured by a notch in the lower end of the forward serpent and a pair of rivets. The large *antha* on the crown of the skull is pierced in the top and probably held a streamer of horse-hair.

The immensely ornate character of the later field head-pieces, which were obviously of very costly manufacture, when compared to contemporary infantry pieces, shows the increasing importance of the cavalry as an independent field force, rather that the mere guardians of a legion's flanks.

The manufacture of deep iron cavalry helmets of plainer type clearly continued at the same time, though with some alterations as against the earlier pattern. The cheek-guards were made into a single element, which

149

Bronze helmet of Cavalry Sports type 'G', found at Heddernheim, Germany. The helmet is tinned all over, except for the decorated areas, which are left bronze. Manufactured in the late second to early third century AD. In the collection of the Frankfurt Museum.

Iron cavalry helmet of Romano-Sassanian type, based on fragments of a skull-piece found at Burgh Castle, Great Yarmouth, England, and a contemporary helmet from Berkasovo, Yugoslavia. This reconstruction by the author represents an alternative type of trooper's head-piece to that shown in colour on p. 154.

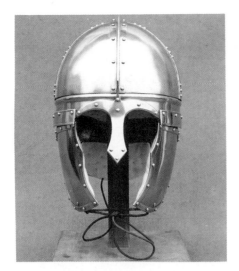

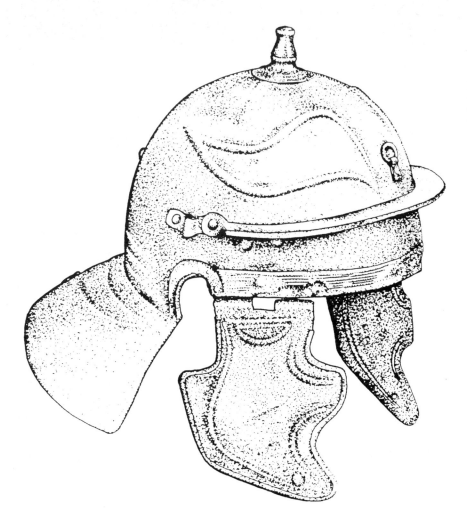

Bronze legionary helmet of Imperial Gallic type 'I', found at *Aquincum*, near Budapest. Despite the Gallic classification, this helmet was probably of Italian make. Manufactured in the late third quarter of the first century AD. In the collection of the Aquincum Museum, Budapest.

PLATE 20   Flavius Valerius Constantius enters *Londinium* after the defeat of Gaius Allectus in Britain, AD 296

The helmet of Constantius is based on the specimen No. 1 from Berkasovo in Yugoslavia, a head-piece in a remarkably good state of preservation. The helmet is of iron with a gilded silver skinning and inlaid glass ornaments to represent jewels. Coin portraits of Emperors sometimes include a helmet of this pattern. His body defence is of lamellar armour; a form of defensive armour which was even then of considerable antiquity, having been used by the Assyrians; examples of Assyrian lamellar plates are in the collection of the British Museum.

Some of the Roman plates are very small, measuring approximately 2 cm (about 1 in) in length; such fine work was no doubt confined to the corselets of the officer class.

The officer who is wearing a helmet with gilded silver skinning, based on an example from Deurne in Holland, also wears a corselet of *lamellae*, but not of such fine construction and left in plain bronze instead of being silvered.

The ordinary troopers wear helmets based on the remains of an iron skull-piece found at Burgh Castle, near Great Yarmouth, England. Because of their plain iron construction, only one fragmentary example of the cavalry head-pieces of the lower order is known at this time; however, subsequent finds and possibly re-identification of existing objects in the possession of museums may alter this position. The trooper wears a long coat of *squamae* similar to that of a *cataphractarius*, based on a relief on the Arch of Galerius which shows mid-arm-length sleeves. The relief also shows a helmet of the Burgh Castle type in fairly accurate detail and a large circular shield.

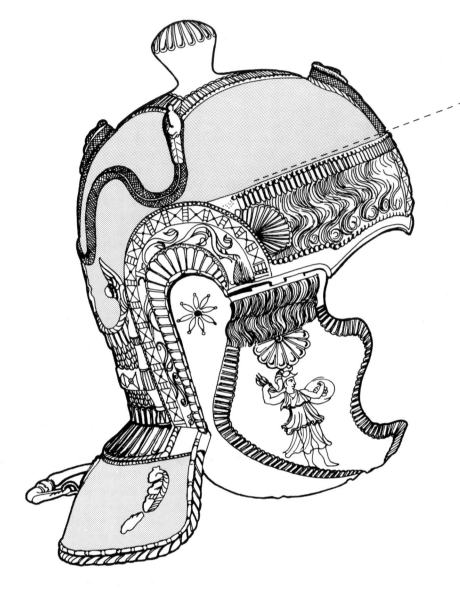

Iron helmet of Auxiliary Cavalry type 'H', found at Heddernheim, Germany. The piece is heavily decorated with thin bronze sheet and serpents. The helmet originally had a peak-plate, now lost. This fine specimen dates from the third century AD. In the collection of the Frankfurt Museum.

Iron cavalry helmet of Romano-Sassanian type, based on fragments of a skull-piece found at Burgh Castle, Great Yarmouth, England, and contemporary pieces from Berkasovo, Yugoslavia. Late third to fourth century AD.

was not attached to the skull-piece with hinges, but was simply tucked under the brow edge and then strapped behind the nape. The triple-reeded applied bronze plates were no longer used and the ear-guards were worked out from the iron skull. A specimen of such a skull-piece was found at Osterburken and is now in the Mannheim Museum.

In the same manner as the helmets of the infantry, the second half of the third century AD saw the introduction of an entirely new method of manu-facture of cavalry helmets. The construction of those helmets was more complex, generally, than those of the infantry, the skull comprising six carefully shaped plates, joined together with a comb and a horizontal band partially inserted inside the lower edge to give greater depth. At the front, an eyebrow and nasal piece was attached with rivets, the band being cut away to coincide with the arches of the brows.

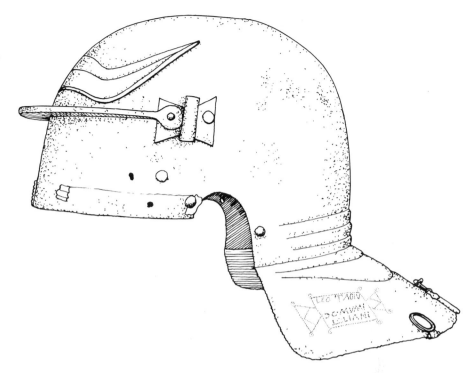

Bronze helmet skull recovered from the river Rhine at Mainz. This helmet was probably made at the same time as the complete specimen from *Aquincum* (p. 152) and may have looked very similar. In the collection of the Germanisches Nationalmuseum, Nuremberg.

The cheek-guards, like those of the infantry, were suspended by means of internal leather 'hinges', the major difference being that all the cavalry pieces were fitted with hinge cover-plates, which obscured the necessary gap between the skull and cheek-guards. The neck-guards, instead of being suspended below the level of the skull, overlapped it and were secured to the band by two leathers which passed through the flange of the neck-guard, to be fastened on the outside with buckles. This rendered the neck-guard removable for stowage; the infantry cheek and neck-guards simply folded inside the skull.

The author's two reconstructions of cavalry troopers' iron helmets of the period are based on fragments discovered in a pit on the site of the fort known as Burgh Castle, near Great Yarmouth, England; the only known remains of such a helmet to be found at this time (see opposite and p. 151). Unfortunately, since there were no definitely identifiable remains of the cheek and neck-guard plates belonging to the skull fragments, those shown are hypothetical, but are consistent with the forms of plates known from contemporary pieces.

The helmets of this period which appear from their ornate finish to have belonged to officers have survived in greater numbers than those which belonged to the ordinary soldiers. The reason for this disparity lies in the fact that helmets of the officer class were usually furnished with a skinning of gilded or plain silver sheet, which either protected the underlying iron, or, where the iron has completely disappeared, the skinning has survived.

Bibliography

Books

Allen, Bernard M., *Augustus Caesar*, London, 1937.

Baker, G.P., *Augustus*, London, 1937.

Connolly, P., *The Roman Army*, London, 1975.

Connolly, P., *Greece and Rome at War*, London, 1981.

Cottrell, L., *The Great Invasion*, London and Southampton, 1958.

Evans, R.F., *Legions of Imperial Rome*, New York, 1980.

Grant, M., *The History of Rome*, London, 1978.

Grant, M. and Pottinger, D., *Romans*, Edinburgh, 1960.

Klawans, Z.H., *Roman Imperial Coins*, Racine, Wisconsin, 1963.

Klumbach, H., *Römische Helme aus Niedergermanien*, Cologne, 1974.

Klumbach, H., *Spätrömische Gardehelme*, Munich, 1973.

Mommsen, T., *The History of Rome*, translated by W.P. Dickson, introduction by E.A. Freeman, 1868.

Robinson, H.R., *The Armour of Imperial Rome*, London, 1975.

Robinson, H.R., *What the Soldiers Wore on Hadrian's Wall*, Newcastle upon Tyne, 1976.

Webster, G., *Boudica — The British Revolt Against Rome*, London, 1978.

Webster, G., *The Roman Invasion of Britain*, London, 1980.

Webster, G., *Rome Against Caratacus*, London, 1981.

Webster, G., *The Roman Imperial Army*, 3rd edition, London, 1985.

Yadin, Y., *Masada*, London, 1968.

Ancient Literary Sources

Penguin Classics:

Caesar, *The Conquest of Gaul*, translated by S.A. Handford, 1951.

Josephus, *The Jewish War*, translated by G.A. Williamson, 1959.

Sallust, *The Jugurthine War*, translated by S.A. Handford, 1963.

Suetonius, *The Twelve Caesars*, translated by Robert Graves, 1957.

Tacitus, *The Annals of Imperial Rome*, translated by M. Grant, 1956.

Tacitus, *The Histories*, translated by K. Wellesley, 1964.

Other Sources

Papers and notes selected from *Britannia*, published by the Society for the Promotion of Roman Studies, London.

Frere, S.S. and St Joseph, J.K., 'The Roman Fortress at Longthorpe', Vol. V, 1974.

Buckland, P., 'A First-century Shield from Doncaster', Vol. IX, 1978.

Griffiths, N.A., 'A Gladius from Dorset, in the Ashmolean Museum', Vol. X, 1979.

Johnson, S., 'Late Roman Helmet from Burgh Castle', Vol. XI, 1980.

Jackson, R., 'The Chester Gladiator Rediscovered', Vol. XIV, 1983.

Jenkins, I., 'A Group of Silvered Horse Trappings from Xanten', Vol. XVI, 1985.

All the reconstructions of Roman military equipment shown in this volume are examples of the author's craft. Museums, public bodies and private individuals interested in purchasing material of that nature, may contact the author by writing to the following address: Michael Simkins, 9a, Priory Road, West Bridgford, Nottingham NG2 5HU, UK.

Index